FINNIGAN'S GUIDE TO THE OTTAWA VALLEY

FINNIGAN'S GUIDE
to the
OTTAWA VALLEY

*A Cultural & Historical
Companion*

Joan Finnigan

Quarry Press

The author would like to thank Roderick MacKenzie for the idea of this book,
as well as Betty Corson, the editor of this book.
Versions of Chapters 1, 2, 3, and 7 have appeared in *Ottawa Magazine*.

CANADIAN CATALOGUING IN PUBLICATION DATA

Finnigan, Joan, 1925–
Finnigan's guide to the Ottawa Valley

Includes index.
ISBN 0-919627-82-X

1. Ottawa River Valley (Quebec and Ont.) — Description and travel.
2. Ottawa River Valley (Quebec and Ont.) — History and criticism.
I. Title.

FC2775.F46 1988   917.13'8044   C88-090283-3
F1054.09.F46 1988

All photographs by Joan Finnigan, except as noted.
Maps by Margot Finley.
Design and imaging by ECW Production Services, Sydenham, Ontario.
Printed by Tri-Graphic Printing, Ottawa.

Published by Quarry Press, Inc., Box 1061, Kingston, Ontario K7L 4Y5

Distributed by University of Toronto Press
5201 Dufferin Street, Downsview, Ontario M3H 5T8

Contents

Introduction 6

Chapter 1 Ferryboat Junkets on the Ottawa River 11

Chapter 2 Glengarry Days 39

Chapter 3 Through Lovely Lanark 61

Chapter 4 Aylmer: The Leisure Capital Within the Capital 77

Chapter 5 Up the Pontiac! 107

Chapter 6 Around and About Renfrew 139

Chapter 7 Along the Opeongo Line 169

Chapter 8 Pembroke and the White-Water Country 199

Appendix Tourist Information Centres 223

Index Place Names 225

Introduction

Finnigan's Guide to the Ottawa Valley is a somewhat unconventional tour book not only for what it includes but also for what it excludes. For travellers looking to find information on accommodation facilities (hotels, motels, campgrounds, bed and breakfast) or on recreational facilities (fishing holes, boat launches, hiking trails, hunting hot spots), Finnigan's Guide has little to offer other than a few passing asides and an appendix listing provincial, regional, and local tourist information centres. Before heading out on any one of the eight tours described in this Guide, travellers are advised to write or call these information centres for detailed maps and brochures. Finnigan's Guide is also short on precise details, such as hours of operation for the various museums and heritage buildings noted along the way of each tour. Since many of these sites are operated seasonally and indeed unpredictably (as befits the character of the Ottawa Valley), hours of operation could not be pinned down, nor could the proprietors, for that matter.

What Finnigan's Guide includes, what makes it especially rich for would-be travellers, is information about the history and cultural heritage of the Ottawa Valley. Over the past 10 years while working on my four oral histories of the Valley (Some of the Stories I Told You Were True, Laughing All the Way Home, Legacies, Legends & Lies, and Tell Me Another Story), I have travelled thousands of miles up and down its highways and byways, its concession roads and its overgrown trails, never failing to glory in its beauty, both pastoral and pristine, and oftentimes almost shedding a tear for its singularly rich heritage and historic sites, which are now so often ruthlessly and insensitively destroyed, mutilated, and even burned down to save on taxes. I do indeed feel at times that "there was no help for it, seeing that my country was not born at all." How a society treats its children, its older people, and its heritage are three indicators of its maturity. And very often I feel that although the Ottawa Valley may have been "born," it has certainly never matured.

And so this little tour book grew out of a desire to share with everyone the beauty and the history of my beloved Valley and to make people who are lucky enough to live in the Valley, or to visit it, aware of their responsibility to preserve its rich heritage resources, such as the Opeongo Line, Herron's Mills, Balaclava, the timber barons' castles of the lumbering towns — Pembroke, Renfrew, Arnprior — and the precious pioneer log buildings that give the Ottawa Valley its distinctive character.

To offer the reading traveller or the travelling reader a stronger flavour of the character of the Valley, I have spiced each tour with 'stories' — humorous tall and even true tales of Valley life past and present told to me by the folk as I travelled these trails. The Ottawa Valley is as rich in stories as it is in history. Don't hesitate to stop along the way and hear a tale or two told by some of the best storytellers in the world.

My aim in writing such an unconventional tour guide is to offer the traveller a cultural and historical companion whether the traveller actually sets out by automobile to tour the Valley or whether the traveller sits in an armchair and imagines such voyages. If more people go on these voyages of discovery, whether real or imaginary, and find themselves enriched by an increased awareness of the very special qualities of the Ottawa Valley, then some of the goals of this guide will have been achieved.

Joan Finnigan
Hartington, Ontario

7

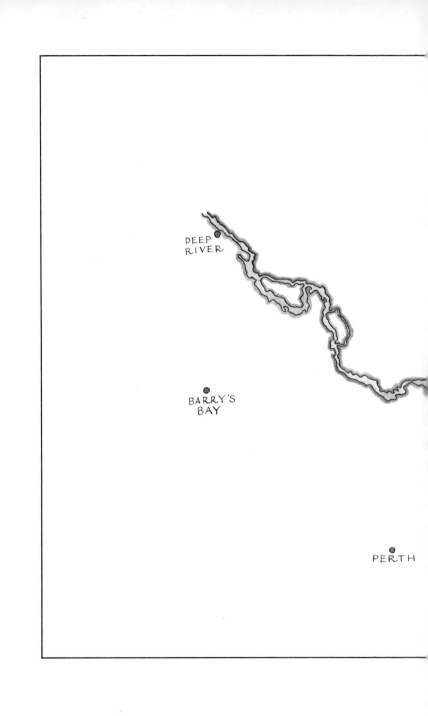

DEEP
RIVER

BARRY'S
BAY

PERTH

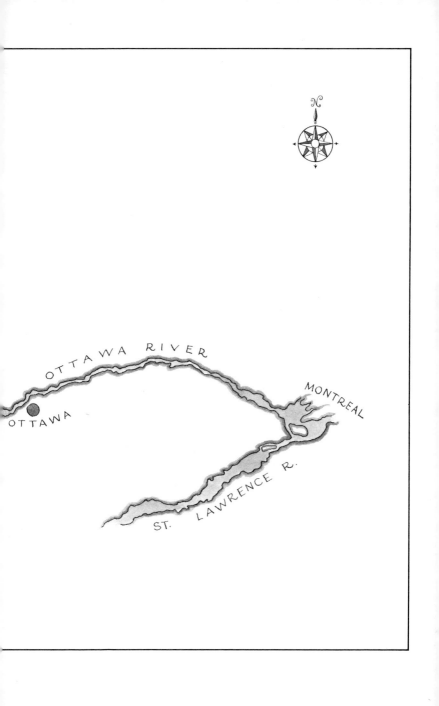

Finnigan's Guide
to the
Ottawa Valley

Ottawa, the capital city of Canada, is generally the hub from which the eight tours in this book set out. Each tour is planned to last one day, but the book is arranged to offer grander excursion possibilities. For example, a weekend tour could begin with the ferryboat junkets described in Chapter 1 ("Ferryboat Junkets on the Ottawa River") and end with a trip through Glengarry County, described in Chapter 2 ("Glengarry Days"). Similar weekend packages could be created by combining other chapters. For the truly adventuresome traveller, the *Guide* offers an eight-day-week excursion: begin with the ferryboat tour back and forth across the Ottawa River and end with a white-water rafting trip down the Ottawa. The possibilities for side trips along the way are endless.

CHAPTER 1

FERRYBOAT   JUNKETS
on the
OTTAWA RIVER

Preamble

I f you have a passion for ferryboats, consider yourself a boating buff, want your children to experience the Ottawa Valley
by water, or simply want to get a feel or a sense of the mighty
Ottawa River for yourself, why not take a ferryboat junket? Like
a walking tour of Aylmer or a driving tour of the Opeongo Line,
ferryboating is a refreshing way to see part of the Ottawa Valley.

Fifty years ago you could have crossed the Ottawa at a dozen
points between Hawkesbury and Deux Rivières and spent a week
ferryboat touring. Today, only five ferries remain, and four of
them discussed in this chapter will give you the flavour of this
mode of travel:

1. *The Quyon–Mohr's Landing Ferry*, running continuously
   from March to November
2. *The Masson–Cumberland Ferry*, running year round
3. *The Thurso–Rockland Ferry*, running year round
4. *The Pointe Fortune–Carillon Ferry*, running summer season
   only

11

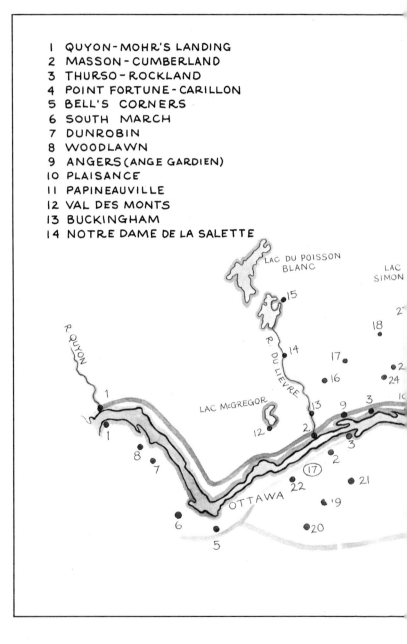

1 QUYON-MOHR'S LANDING
2 MASSON-CUMBERLAND
3 THURSO-ROCKLAND
4 POINT FORTUNE-CARILLON
5 BELL'S CORNERS
6 SOUTH MARCH
7 DUNROBIN
8 WOODLAWN
9 ANGERS (ANGE GARDIEN)
10 PLAISANCE
11 PAPINEAUVILLE
12 VAL DES MONTS
13 BUCKINGHAM
14 NOTRE DAME DE LA SALETTE

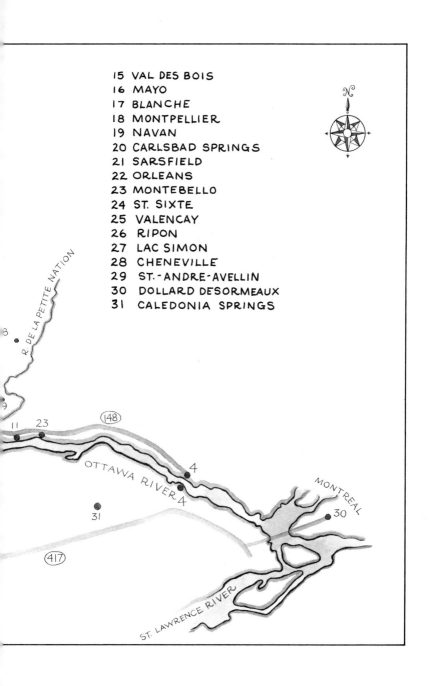

15 VAL DES BOIS
16 MAYO
17 BLANCHE
18 MONTPELLIER
19 NAVAN
20 CARLSBAD SPRINGS
21 SARSFIELD
22 ORLEANS
23 MONTEBELLO
24 ST. SIXTE
25 VALENCAY
26 RIPON
27 LAC SIMON
28 CHENEVILLE
29 ST.-ANDRE-AVELLIN
30 DOLLARD DESORMEAUX
31 CALEDONIA SPRINGS

N

R. DE LA PETITE NATION

8

9

11 23

148

OTTAWA RIVER

4

31

417

MONTREAL

30

ST. LAWRENCE RIVER

If you are travelling *en famille* it is advisable to pack a picnic and take along swimming things. For adults a number of very fine dining places are clustered around the two ferries in the Lower Ottawa Valley, so it's best to pack your credit cards or a hefty wallet. And for the Lower Valley, also include your French-English dictionary and your high school French. Many of the people in the little Québècois towns tucked along the route do not speak English. If they can't, they will usually find you someone who does, so you are rarely really in trouble.

Before the junket, sit down and study the map to decide whether you want to begin your journey in the more sophisticated populated ferry-crossing areas of the Lower Ottawa River or in the more scenic *au naturel* landscape of the Quyon ferry on the Upper Ottawa. In essence, you will be making figure-eights of your own choice and plotting on this ferryboat junket.

Quyon–Mohr's Landing Ferry

In Ottawa, take Island Park Drive and cross the Champlain Bridge and, turning left at the stoplights, travel up the Eardley Road, Highway No. 148, to Quyon, where the ferryboat signs are prominent. You can have a holiday beer at Gavan's famous hotel in Quyon on the main street, although the Quyon Fiddlers or Singing Gavans may not be performing before noon.

Quyon Beach is sandy, clear, and uncrowded, making it a fine swimming and picnicking place for the family. Across the river at Mohr's Landing is a heritage log house where you can have lunch or tea, specially prepared for you.

HISTORY

According to notes left in the papers of W.H. Mohr, descendant of a first family and storekeeper and lumber operator at Quyon, the first Quyon ferryboat was "only a rowboat," improved upon later by "rowboats tied together." This conveyance was succeeded by a steam-operated ferry owned by Augustus Davis.

QUYON-MOHR'S LANDING FERRY

*One of the narrowest stretches of the Ottawa River is at Quyon,
making it ideal for a ferry crossing. This photograph shows the first
Quyon ferry, a horse-powered cage ferry. The horses circled on a
wooden platform above a steel cable attached to an anchor. Today the
ferry at Quyon is somewhat differently powered.*

In 1900, for some reason or another, that ferryboat was replaced by a horse-tamper ferry built and operated by William McLean. Two horses walked around and around, turning a cog gear that operated the paddles on the boat. Evidently the animals did this for four years until William Mohr, Jr., for some reason or another, built and operated a third Quyon ferry, this one also horse-tamper driven.

From 1905 until 1920 William McLean and his son Angus ran the horse ferry. Angus McLean continued to run this ferry until about 1926, when he changed over to a gasoline-engine-propelled boat with steel floats. And this he operated for 50 years, becoming a legend on the Ottawa River. Faithful as the North Star, the doughty Scotsman ferried rivermen and shantymen, farmers with animals and produce on their way to market and country fairs, natives coming home for family weddings, hearses crossing the river to graveyards, strangers and tourists, roistering young people looking for the next party, penniless prodigal sons returning to the Valley on foot, prodigal daughters fleeing the Valley on their way to pie in the sky in California.

Writing an obit for the Quyon ferry in the *Ottawa Journal* on October 27, 1956, reporter James Purdie recorded: "Patches were few at first, but dotted the decks in later years. Hulls were worn thin while the pontoons went on and on. The big side paddles churned out a million miles. Rivermen of Quyon are asking if a motor can ever be built again to equal the one in that ferry. It's burning a little oil now, and there's a catch in its purr, but the motor is only on its third set of rings after forty summers.

"Her frankly ugly lines, broken in spots by dry rot and weather, recall romance, adventure and reliability for three generations."

Like the Spirit Boatmen of the Sky, so often seen by the early rivermen and settlers in the Valley, Angus McLean might be running his cantankerous and invincible old boat across the Ottawa to this day if it weren't for Hurricane Hazel. The storm whipped Angus McLean and his ferryboat down the river several miles off course, bringing changes of current that were too much for the two old veterans of the river. But McLean brought his boat upstream to Mohr's Landing without so much as harming a hair on the heads of the cargo of cows he was carrying at the time. However, the boat was irreparably damaged.

Besides Captain McLean, the Quyon ferry was serviced by two other old faithfuls. For 37 years Joseph Kilbride, former Gillies shantyman and riverman, manned the sweep, a huge oar by which the ferry was steered into dock. Despite the clumsy sweep, Kilbride could dock the ferry without the slightest difficulty and within the margin of a toothpick.

In 1956, following Angus McLean's death, the ferry was leased by Ed McColgan of Quyon, descendant of one of the first families there. Like the Mohrs, the McColgans went into lumber and, like the Mohrs, McColgan houses still stand in the village today.

DIRECTIONS

Once you cross on the Quyon ferry to Mohr's Landing on the Ontario side of the river, you can follow the signs to the major Highway, No. 417 or, if you prefer the byways, you can travel across the peninsula along the Ottawa River, via the towns of Woodlawn, Dunrobin, and South March, into Ottawa, or via the towns of Galetta, Kinburn, Carp, South March, and Bells Corners, into Ottawa. Both routes lead to the Queensway through Ottawa to the next ferryboat. Cross the Island Park Bridge or the Interprovincial Bridge to Hull, go through on Highway No. 148 to Gatineau Point, and then along the fabled North Shore of the Ottawa River to Masson. A number of winding scenic routes Highway Nos. 366, 309, 315, 317 run north off No. 348 to little, untouched villages, beautiful lakes, mountain splendours, and parks for stopovers. You'll also find craft shops and a few good restaurants along the way.

Masson–Cumberland Ferry

The villages of the North Shore give the traveller a wonderful flavour of old Quebec, for along this route remain the narrow riverfront farms, original buildings, some "first" log houses, mansard farmhouses, and some early "stones" (stone houses). All along this route vintage villages like Angers, Plaisance, Papineauville, are enhanced by untouched Québècois houses and dominated by huge Roman Catholic churches. The major industry of the area is manifest in the "Mountains of Wood" along the highway at mills at Gatineau Point, Thurso, Masson, Buckingham where the Maclaren dynasty, the last of the great lumbering companies of the Ottawa Valley, still operates two mills.

HISTORY

The North Shore route is the old stagecoach trail from Ottawa to Montreal. About 1840 a regular stagecoach route was established between Bytown and Montreal. In addition to the mail, some passengers were carried. W.H. Cluff in his *Reminiscences of Winter Travel on the Ottawa* remembers as a young boy of 11 following the stagecoach trail, accompanying his father, a prominent builder in Bytown, to the glass works at Como for a shipment of glass to be used in a new building on Sparks Street, then a muddy thoroughfare without any parking problems.

Cluff describes another early mode of transportation common in the early days along the North Shore: "Sometimes stocks would run short towards the end of the winter and large quantities of goods would be carted from Montreal in sleighs known as *traineux*. These were horsed by splendid French-Canadian ponies strong, hardy and tough — in strings of 15 or 20 sleighs with a teamster for each three or four."

Cluff wrote that, as a young boy, he would sometimes be awakened on a cold winter's night in Bytown by the sound of the teamsters singing on the trail a *chanson* perhaps dedicated to some black-eyed belle of the river for whose smile the great Joe Montferrand and lesser champions had fought.

The old trail left Bytown via New Edinburgh and headed for Gatineau Point, continuing along the North Shore beyond Kettle Island to the first stopping-place, 10 miles beyond Bytown. Buckingham Landing marked the second 10-mile stretch. Below Buckingham Landing the road continued for another 10 miles along the North Shore to the third tavern, kept by an old-timer named Whittemore. Here usually ended the first day's journey, for Whittemore kept a popular place. At nightfall his yard was usually crowded with conveyances, and, after the horses had been stabled, the teamsters made for the great log fire and swapped their tall tales of the Ottawa Valley.

Following breakfast at Dole's stopping-place, eight miles further down the road, the next break in the journey was Cummings'

Hotel (probably one of those Cummings from Cumberland and environs). Next respite was Jamor's stopping-place at the Papineau Seigneury. Here the road crossed over to the South Shore, to the Upper Canada side of the Ottawa at Oak Point, continuing through Plantagenet and Alfred to Hawkesbury, which in those days, as centre of the Hamilton brothers' lumbering enterprise, was one of the most important communities on the Ottawa.

The second night of the trip was usually spent at Kirby's celebrated stopping-place six miles below Hawkesbury. Early the next morning, always before breakfast, the caravan moved on to Pointe Fortune, seven miles distant.

Ten miles down the Lake of Two Mountains was Schneider's Point, later called Hudson. Three miles below Hudson was the Cluff's destination, Como, site of a glass factory founded there in 1847 by George Desbarats and S. Derbyshire. The last night of the Cluff's stagecoach journey was spent at Lachine.

SIDE TRIP NORTH UP HIGHWAY NO. 366

Perkins Mills (Val-des-Monts)

From Templeton, just outside of Gatineau Point, Highway No. 366 makes its way north to Ste-Rose-de-Lima, thence northeast from the village to Perkins Mills (Val Des Monts), the site of Williams's water-powered grist mill on the Blanche River, dating from 1860. Here coarse grains are still ground for the community farmers; until 1965 wool from the hill-farms flocks was carded here.

Perkins Mills is named for John Adam Perkins, who built a sawmill here about 1845. Shortly afterward, when Bishop Guiges of Ottawa visited in 1842, it was decided to build the first chapel.

McGregor Lake

Largely owned by summer cottagers and off limits to travellers and tourists, the north shore of McGregor Lake is also the summer residence of the Scholastic St. Joseph of the Oblate Order. Young missionaries-in-training maintain trails and portage paths linking the lakes and making it possible to reach Lac du Poisson Blanc going from McGregor Lake via the Lièvre River by canoe.

Angers (Ange-Gardien)

Back on Highway No. 148, Angers is a charming little village, visited by the itinerant missionary, the Reverend John Brady, as early as 1851. The first chapel was built in 1854. The legend here is that Métis leader Louis Riel sheltered in Ange-Gardien during one of his secret visits in 1873 and 1874, when he was a fugitive from justice. A certain patriot, M. Moncian, was said to have sheltered Riel in a house that has now disappeared. Riel was also supposed to have been given refuge in Gatineau Point and Hull.

Masson

Masson, along with Buckingham, three miles to the north, is the centre of Maclaren country. Masson is a busy mill town and site of the huge Maclaren saw and pulp mills, begun here in 1929. From the point where the Lièvre River enters the Ottawa there is a deep channel a mile and a half long, up which steamers in the early days would make their way. The head of this channel was called the Rafting Basin; two timber slides that ran four miles down from the mills of Buckingham and Ross terminated here. Here on the flatlands of the glacial till of the Ottawa River lumber and timber were piled to dry before shipment. Although the logs are considerably smaller these days, the 'Mountains of Wood' remain, turning the wheels of the economy. Logically, almost all the houses on the North Shore of the Ottawa are made of wood, usually white frame. The Lièvre River used to be called La Rivière Aux Lièvres, after the snowshoe rabbit. One of Ottawa poet Archibald Lampman's most popular works is "Morning on the Lièvre," later made into one of the National Film Board's most internationally renowned canoe films of the same name.

SIDE TRIP NORTH UP HIGHWAY NO. 309

At Masson, turn north toward the mountain, following Highway No. 309, and drive the three miles to Buckingham, the site of another Maclaren mill. No. 309 parallels the beautiful, dark Lièvre

River, providing splendid vistas of waters and mountains through picturesque towns such as Notre-Dame-de-la-Salette and Val-des-Bois.

Buckingham

Justus Smith named the township and the town after the county in England when he came in from Montreal in 1823. He brought with him a group of workers and built a sawmill at a cascade on the Lièvre. In 1824 Smith sold to Baxter Bowman (later one of the partners in the Bowman and McGill lumbering company). Levi Bigelow, also arriving in 1824, opened a store to serve the growing lumbering community, then built another sawmill next to Baxter's on the east side of the falls. The settlement grew so quickly that the first chapel was built in 1835. Again, like so many tiny, growing settlements on the North Shore, it was first served by the ubiquitous itinerant priest, Father John Brady, who spent his winters ministering to the shanties in the bush, where most of the men of the countryside went to work in the winters.

The Bigelow mill passed through several sets of hands after 1850, first in 1851 to Ross Brothers and then in 1901 to the James Maclaren Company Ltd. The Maclarens bought the Bowman mill in 1864. Buckingham was quickly advanced by its two major functions as a mill town and as an entrepôt for men, supplies, and teams going northwards to the shanties.

There are a great many old buildings of special importance and charm in Buckingham.

The John Thompson House

Sometimes called the Kenney house, this home was built for John Thompson, who from 1853 to 1869 managed the old Bigelow sawmill at Hawkesbury for the Hamilton brothers, major timber barons. This white frame Victorian, dating from 1853, sits on a curved drive right on Main Street, in estate grounds on the river.

Commercial Building

Built on the northeast corner of Main and Church streets in 1841, this building was the headquarters, office, and store of Ross

Brothers, which operated the Bigelow sawmill from 1869 to 1901. Before that, it may have been Levi Bigelow's store.

The Stacey–McNaughton House

This house, at 133 Joseph Street, was built in the 1850s for George Stacey, bookkeeper for either Baxter Bowman or the Maclaren Company. Later Archibald McNaughton operated a temperance hotel in the building.

170–172 Joseph Street

John Higginson, who came to the mill site on the Lièvre with Levi Bigelow in 1824, built this place.

Sadly, no great Maclaren Houses remain in Maclaren country. They built three large brick houses in Buckingham but demolished all the stately residences over the years, even one known as Neralcam Hall or "The Castle," an impressive 1896 slate-roofed Victorian mansion with 11 fireplaces and the entire upper half given over to a ballroom.

❡ STORY

"The Battle at Buckingham"

During the peak of the lumbering period in the Ottawa Valley, 1850–1900, in the spring drives, rafts of timber ran past these North Shore settlements in such continuous succession that they must have resembled a caravan. Consequently, the legends, tall tales, folktales of the shantymen, rivermen, lumber barons abound here. One of the great stories of the legendary riverman, Joseph Montferrand, known in the English bastardization as Joe Mufferaw, took place in a stopping-place at Buckingham.

Martin Hennessy of Pembroke, foreman for one of the lumber companies of the era, was a singing, fast-swinging giant of a man. He was also bodyguard for Peter Aylen, leader of the Shiners, a vigilante group of Irishmen dedicated to driving the French Canadians out of the lumbering business and taking over the jobs for themselves. Hennessy ached to encounter Montferrand, the great champion of the French Canadians.

It is said that Hennessy was constantly composing and singing a eulogy to himself, in which one of the verses went:

"Oh, Montferrand of the strong foot
Will hear from me.
I'll hunt him and catch him,
And he'll fall like a tree."

Hennessy's chance finally came when Joe, on business for Bowman and McGill, went into a work camp near Buckingham, Quebec. He was wearing a new beaver hat given to him by his boss, Mr. Bowman. When his work was completed, Joe as usual, stopped by the village inn. There he found himself in the presence of 20 Shiners, with Martin Hennessy amongst them. The men had been drinking before Joe arrived, and, although the banter about his classy hat was friendly at first, it quickly became abusive. Finally Hennessy strode up and squashed Joe's fine hat.

"*En garde! À toute fair!*" Joe cried, springing into action.

With these words the barroom doors were all closed by Hennessy's men.

Joe realized that, in a room full of hostile people, he had to measure his movements very carefully. When he moved slightly out of the ring, or backed up, Hennessy's men rained kicks on him from the rear so hard that he retained traces of them all his life. They went 15 rounds before Montferrand smashed Hennessy "like a baked apple." Hennessy, always slow to provoke a *Canadien* after the Battle at Buckingham, was killed a few years later in a pistol duel in a tavern.

✳

SIDE TRIP NORTH UP HIGHWAY NO. 315

At Buckingham, in the heart of the town, you can turn right off onto Highway No. 315 and make a side trip into the mountain toward Mayo, Blanche, and Montpellier.

Mayo

A tiny hamlet, set in a green valley, surrounded by mountains, reminiscent of the Old Sod, Mayo was settled by the "Haleys, Baileys, and Dalys of Mayo" in the 1850s. It is distinguished by a very ancient graveyard, which, like the one at Brudenell on the Opeongo Line, is 100 percent full of dead Irishmen, and by one of the few *wooden* Roman Catholic churches in the country (see also the one at Notre-Dame-de-la-Salette). In a separate wing of this church is the only English Roman Catholic shrine in Quebec. Each year thousands of pilgrims visit this holy place, some of them seeking — and finding — miracles.

Naturally, the church is painted green and white.

Cumberland

Now return to Masson on Highway No. 148 and cross the river on the ferry to Upper Canada. This is one point at which you can savour the Ottawa region again, travelling from Masson by ferry-boat to Cumberland, a settlement almost as old as Hull.

Abijah Dunning and his four sons landed here in 1801; Amable Foubert arrived in 1807 and established a fur-trading post. John Munroe, Walter Beckwith, G.C. Dunning, and William Wilson followed. By 1880 Cumberland was the chief commercial town of Cumberland Township, and a regular stopping-place for all boats on the Ottawa, as well as for all the shantymen moving downriver on the Drive.

Cumberland, at Highway Nos. 34 and 17, has a goodly number of heritage houses, chief amongst them the *William Wilson House*. A native of Edinburgh, Scotland, Wilson grew up in Montreal and became a Crown Timber Agent in Buckingham. In 1848 he moved to Cumberland, where he opened a general store. Wilson founded a family prominent in the affairs of the capital, including the Honourable Cairine Wilson, first woman to be appointed to the Senate.

On Main Street, wrapped in two-storey verandas with dormer windows set in a mansard roof, is the residence of *Dr. James Ferguson*, physician in the area for no less than 60 years from 1861 to 1921.

On the outskirts of Cumberland to the south is Calvary in *French Hill*, a landmark cross rising against the skyline of this flat country and magnified by the flat terrain.

On Highway No. 34, east of Cumberland, about a quarter-mile out of the village, is the *Cumberland Museum*, an historic village composed of 10 buildings, all moved onto the site, including a museum in progress, train station, church, school, and several outstanding private residences typical of the lifestyle, occupation, and industries of Cumberland Township and the Lower Ottawa Valley.

Navan

Perhaps you would like to meander the byways through the lush flatlands of this farming area and the little towns that stand to the east of Ottawa as reminders of early settlements: Navan, Sarsfield, Carlsbad Springs, Orléans, Sulphur Springs, Caledon Springs, and Rockland.

Like Cumberland, Navan is an early town — its old graveyard verifies this and was settled by McKinnons, Murrays, Grimeses, Alexanders, McCulloughs, Rathwells, and Wilsons. In 1848 Edward Code came to Navan with more Cummingses, his cousins, William and Thomas. Settlers John and Michael O'Meara named Navan after their hometown in Ireland.

Carlsbad Springs

When farmer Daniel Eastman found a bubbling spring on his property, he and his neighbours set to drinking it, and found it valuable as a purgative. In 1864 Eastman built his hotel and called his new health spa Cathartick. Some Ottawa entrepreneurs decided to capitalize on the healing waters, and in 1870 they built a much grander hotel called Dominion Springs. Some of its most eminent patrons were Lady MacNab from Dundurn Castle in Hamilton, her daughter, Sophia, and Sir John A. Macdonald.

After the Dominion Springs Hotel burned in 1876, James Boyd built a large frame guest house, which survives today in derelict condition. Apart from the healing waters and the sulphur baths, the Boyd family dispensed — even in those days — health foods, including special breads, sugar, honey, and other dietary items prescribed for all ages from the cradle to the grave.

Sulphur Springs

South of the Queensway, in the Green Creek valley, are the ruins of another of the old health springs found in the area and once the centre of a lively search for the Fountain of Health and Youth. Sulphur water still flows in Green Creek from a rusted pipe into an old hardwood barrel. Since this spring is inside the National Capital Region, the NCC hopes to develop this sulphur spring area into a park and perhaps reactivate some of the springs.

Rockland–Thurso Ferry

You can return to the Quebec side of this tour by taking the Masson–Cumberland ferry that you came on, but if you have the time, the Rockland–Thurso ferry trip is more interesting. Make your way to Rockland (Highway No. 17) and cross the Ottawa River to Thurso. On the North Shore another set of historic sites greets you, including Plaisance, Papineauville, and Montebello Seigneury.

Thurso and Beyond

From Masson, if you choose that crossing, return to Highway No. 148 and proceed to Thurso, named by the first Scottish settlers for their town in the north of Scotland. Thurso is another "Mountain of Wood" mill town. You can side-trip *again*, if you wish, up Highway No. 317 through St-Sixte, Valencay, and Ripon to lovely Lac-Simon, then past Chénéville on Highway No. 321, where there are opportunities for swimming, boating, picnicking, camping, especially at *Centre Touristique* on the eastern shore of the lake. There are about 300 campsites here set in low, wooded hills around Lac Simon with an excellent sandy beach.

Returning to Highway No. 148 via No. 317, at Valencay you come to Bac-Ku, a medium-priced dining room featuring Canadian cuisine and specializing in steak and fish.

Plaisance

Situated on the Petite Nation River, which runs through the Papineau–Montebello Seigneury, Plaisance is as beautiful as its name implies. Above Plaisance to the north, the Petite Nation River tumbles in rock-tangled tumult toward the Ottawa, making a succession of poetic waterfalls, some of which bear the ruins of old mill sites. To the south of Plaisance lies a long grassy peninsula jutting out into the Ottawa, on which is sited Parc Plaisance, again providing the travelling family with camping, swimming, fishing, and boating in the summer; snowmobiling, cross-country skiing, skating, and ice fishing in the winter. Summer visitors may rent rowboats, canoes, and bicycles.

Papineauville

Although the grossly unsuitable picture window is creeping in, the village of Papineauville, like its sibling, Montebello, a few miles down the road, maintains to a high level its French Canadian imprint. Street after street is still lined with houses, both grand and humble, that embody the history of Lower Canada. Both towns deserve a walking tour.

At Papineauville, housed in a *"maison fondée in 1880,"* La Table de Pierre Delahaye is one of those exquisite French cuisine experiences that you should not preclude. Someone once said if you can afford a yacht, you don't ask the price of it. The same applies to M. Delahaye's dining place: if you want the best, I can give you this recommendation, but not the price list for his à la carte menu, his table d'hôte, or his luncheon specials. Suffice it to say that the fresh lobsters are in an immaculate tank outside his kitchen door, and that Delahaye (his name is Norman French) has had 22 years experience as *chef gourmet et gastronomique*, 12 in France, eight in Montreal, and two years as owner-chef of his own business. Calvados is the house specialty. Lobster is one of his gastronomical specials.

✱

SIDE TRIP NORTH UP HIGHWAY NO. 321

At Papineauville, Highway No. 321 turns north, again following the other shore of the Petite Nation River toward Vinoy and the famous "potato country" of Namur. The drive is spectacularly beautiful.

Montebello (The Seigneury de la Petite Nation)

Return to Highway No. 148 and continue east to one of the truly fascinating places along the Ottawa River. Montebello is clearly a grand site, rich in history, rich in taste.

HISTORY

Louis XIV of France, known as the Sun King, was in the habit of giving his supporters large tracts of land in the New World along the St. Lawrence River, and later along the Lower Ottawa River above its entrance to the St. Lawrence near Montreal Island. These gifts of wilderness were called seigneuries, with wonderful names like Grand Vallée Mille-Ils, Deux Montagnes, Laprairie de la Madéleine, de Livry, Beaujeu, Rivière du Loup, Trois Pistoles, Nicholas Roux, Rimouski, Bic, St.-Barnabé, St.-Hyacinthe, and Ramesay.

Noblemen and gentry were most often the recipients of the King's largesse, but occasionally ecclesiasts and the military were included in his generosity. The first owners of the Seigneury of Murray Bays were two Scottish captains, John Naire and Malcolm Fraser, whose kilted men were freezing to death in the Canadian winters until the Ivory Nuns knitted them all long woollen stockings!

Montebello, or the area of La Petite Nation, was first and, for longer than we ever can tell, the land of the Algonquin and Ottawa tribes. In 1674 the West Indies Company of Paris ceded the Seigneurie de la Petite Nation to the first Bishop of New France, François de Montmorency-Laval, famous in history simply as Bishop Laval.

The original deed in which the Petite Nation Seigneury was given to Bishop Laval read in part: "All that extent of land fronting on the Saint Lawrence River in New France about forty-two leagues above Montreal, measuring five leagues in breadth by five leagues in depth, to be taken from the Sault de la Chaudière, commonly called La Petite Nation, going downstream along the road of the Outaouais, to hold in all seigniory and justice the said land together with the lakes and rivers in all its width, including the bed thereof, shoals, isles and islands all along the front of said seigniory, with exclusive right of hunting and fishing in perpetuity on the condition to render foi et hommage every twenty years in the Fort Louis in Quebec with 'Maille d'or' equivalent to eleven livres."

Bishop Laval gave this land to his offspring and heir, the Seminary at Quebec, an educational institution for Roman Catholics existing to this day. Between 1801 and 1803 Notary M.P. Joseph Papineau of Montreal acquired the seigneury of over 1,000 acres, with a riverside frontage from east of the present town of Montebello to Plaisance, roughly five miles by five miles. This gift, it was understood, was in return for Papineau's legal services, although the deed of sale makes mention (probably for legal purposes only) of 1,100 louis as the purchase price.

The first manor house, built in 1805 by colonizer Joseph Papineau on Arosen Island in the Ottawa River, became the nucleus for land settlement and establishment of the little communities that exist today — Montebello, Papineauville, and Plaisance. It was destroyed by fire some 30 years later. Unlike the other seigneuries along the St. Lawrence and the Richelieu, the Seigneury de la Petite Nation was to remain in Papineau hands virtually untouched for well over 100 years, an incomparable hunting and fishing preserve dotted with 65 lakes set in the Laurentian Mountains. There was no encroachment of farmlands to change the landscape.

In 1817 Speaker of the House for Lower Canada Louis-Joseph Papineau purchased the seigneury from his father, while his brother, Denis Benjamin, retained the inland territory around Plaisance. But Louis-Joseph was to take his place in the history of Canada before his return to Montebello in the Rebellions in Upper and Lower Canada of 1837–38; in the tragedy of St.-Eustache; in his flight into exile in the United States, the system of government which he most admired; and then in his flight to Paris, where he became a friend of the Duke of Montebello, son of one of Napoleon's generals. After Papineau was pardoned, he returned to his country, took up his law practice in Montreal again, and gradually turned to the colonization and development of his seigneury.

Manoir Montebello

Like most great heritage houses, the Manoir Montebello was built for a woman. In 1846 Louis-Joseph wrote to a friend: "My wife so abhors the idea of living in the country that to surmount all her repugnances, I have decided to build her the most beautiful house possible."

Construction on the two-turretted seigneury castle began in 1847 and took 50 men three years to build from the stone and wood upon the property. Largely used by the Papineaus as a "summer place," it is today maintained as a museum.

Until 1903 four generations of Papineaus lived in this truly outstanding heritage manor; in 1929 the estate of Westcott-Papineau sold the Manoir and its holdings to the Seigneury Club. This exclusive private club made a number of changes to the building, including modernizing the kitchens, putting in bathrooms, and adding a ballroom. But everything was done with considerable sensitivity to the original architecture. In 1975 the Quebec government declared the Manoir of Louis-Joseph Papineau an historic site, but it would not put up the money required to repair the stonework in the three-storey mansion; consequently it was covered with pink stucco.

Outstanding features of the Manoir Montebello include its gracious architecture, with two large towers, the east one containing the renowned spiral staircase.

From the drawing rooms, sunrooms, and bedrooms on the east can be seen an eight-mile stretch of the Ottawa River. From here the Papineaus could watch the Indian traffic and know without fail, in the days when the river was the only highway, who was arriving by canoe or steamboat, who was coming upriver by foot or on snowshoe in the wintertime. Before Louis-Joseph's death in 1871, when the lumbering industry of the Ottawa River was at its height, the Papineau family could count the rafts of lumber almost in tandem going by on their way to the sailing ships at Montreal and Quebec waiting to transport the precious cargo to England and other markets of the world.

Papineau's tower library, a large, unlovely square tower on the northeast part of the building, across from the tiny stone and brick Papineau chapel (now Christ Church), was built as a "fireproof" repository for Papineau's thousands of books. When I first looked at it, I thought it must be part of a fortification against the enemy: Indians? Americans? But the truth of the matter is that Papineau had once lost his entire library in a fire and did not intend to suffer a second disaster. A covered walkway leads from the library tower to his northside office. Originally, there were walkways on each level with stairs leading to the other floors.

MANOIR MONTEBELLO

Louis-Joseph Papineau built this two-towered seigneury castle for his wife in 1850, after he was pardoned for his activities in the Rebellions of 1837–38. The Manoir Montebello has been converted into a museum featuring Papineau's extensive library, a stunning spiral staircase, and a tiny bell tower which once served as the privy.

A tiny belled tower attached to the house by a protective overhead covering was the fancy outdoor privy in the days before plumbing.

Some original furniture is on view, including a massive period mahogany dining room suite, which was graciously returned to Montebello by some members of the Papineau family who had inherited the furniture but felt it should be in the Manoir when it became a museum. An original cast-iron fireplace was also returned by Papineau descendants. A particularly interesting piece of original furniture is a desk from Florence, Italy, inlaid with 25 cameos. Perhaps a sense of the early grandeur of the Manoir is best conveyed in the Gold Room on the second floor with its original wallpaper, ornate gold curtain accoutrements, original curtains, crystal chandeliers, rococo mirrors.

A glass teahouse overlooking the Ottawa River offers miles of view.

Chateau Montebello: **The Largest Log Castle in the World**

In February 1930, on the riverfront of the Seigneury of Montebello, work was begun on the largest log castle in the world, built for the private membership Seigneury Club and today CP's most prestigious resort hotel, the Chateau Montebello.

HISTORY

The Montreal architect, Harold Lawson, responsible for the design, detailed construction, and structural details of the general buildings at Montebello, gives some idea of the impact on society generated by the creation of the Chateau Montebello:

"The creation of the Seigneury Club was BIG NEWS in 1930. The historical association of the site, its vast acreage that was to serve all sportsmen, its provisions for every known winter and summer sport, the unique log buildings, miles of roads, water supply, and all its physical manifestations combined, provided copy for newspapers all over North America. . . . Staid Canadians, after first recovering from the shock that the largest resort to date was planned for the North Shore of the Ottawa River and the hinterland back of Montebello, were further surprised when the building started on a scale and speed that challenged credulity. . . . That they were all built of logs was a novelty; that they were of enormous size captured the imagination and, that all were being erected with miraculous speed added a fillip to the action — the whole performance, if you will — contained from beginning to end all the drama and interest of a three-ring circus."

The enormous publicity given this architectural achievement attracted crowds from near and far, especially on weekends. From Ottawa, Montreal, Toronto, and places unknown people came by train and car to watch tons of building supplies being drawn in over the CPR spur line to the site; to observe the stonemasons, many of them Scottish, at work on the huge foundations and hexagon fireplace; to ogle 10,000 Western red cedar logs of enormous size being reared and set in to place by hundreds of men, mostly French Canadian, some Scandinavian, employing a log-building technique used in Russian and Scandinavian countries for hundreds of years.

The grand climax was reached on July 1, 1930, when work was completed on the first three buildings the log chateau, the huge garage, and the Cedars, a residence building for the staff of the Seigneury Club, including 53 miles of plumbing and heating pipes, 843 toilet fixtures, 700 radiators, 40 miles of conduit and electrical wiring, as well as 2,100 special hand-wrought fixtures, 1,400 doors, 935 windows, 103 miles of wooden molding, and 18,000 square feet of tile.

✳

Today the Chateau Montebello exists for discriminating private clientele, many of whom consider it the unparalleled place to holiday. As one American traveller told me in an informal chat about the glories of Chateau Montebello, "It is the only place in my life I have stayed where everything was better than the brochure said it would be."

The largest log castle in the world literally provides the guest with not only an inspirational architectural and aesthetically pleasing natural setting, but also a haunting sense of history and a warm, cozy, homey atmosphere, all its rooms and suites running off the "hearth" — the monolithic soaring hexagon-shaped stone fireplace that also provides structural support. The rest is a phantasmagoria of fine cuisine, special events, sporting activities, places for civilized leisure and relaxation, social opportunities.

With more than 70 lakes and countless streams and brooks, as well as the Petite Nation River running through, the 65,000-acre property of the Montebello Seigneury remains a unique wildlife preserve as unspoiled as it was centuries ago. Montebello Properties stocks a number of the lakes with fish, including three species of trout and ouananiche. A nearby hatchery operated by marine biology specialists ensures a steady supply of fish throughout the season.

Completely equipped cabins for hunters and fishermen can be rented throughout the Commandant area on the Salmon River, Mills Lake, Taunton Lake, Commandant Lake, & Sugarbush Lake.

Just 15 miles from the Chateau, at the northern end of Commandant Road, a fully equipped marina serves as the gateway to Commandant Lake. Fishermen and hunters can rent motorboats, canoes, and rowboats. Gasoline, boat, and fishing supplies, including gear, bait, and all accessories, can be bought. Rods and nets can be rented; guides are on hand for hunters and fishermen.

Visitors with their own boats are permitted to use them on the lake for a daily fee and wharfage is available for a fee. Space can be rented for storage of private boats.

The array of sporting activities includes golfing, swimming, bicycling, horseback riding, tennis, badminton, squash, croquet, and a putting green. Horseshoes and volleyball are available at the tennis chalet. There is no charge to registered guests for many of the activities.

Summer activity at Montebello is heightened by a Spring Greek Festival in April, an Hawaiian Festival in July, and Oktoberfest in October. These higher-priced weekends guarantee a continuous round of ethnic festivity, including special menus for all meals, special cocktail receptions, special entertainment, special music for dancing. These are usually booked months in advance.

Winter at Montebello is a time to enjoy cross-country skiing, curling, snowshoeing, skating, sleigh riding, as well as an opportunity to enjoy the indoor pool and its sauna, whirlpool, and exercise room. A lower winter occupancy is boosted betimes by special ski packages for individuals, by ski packages for annual 100-200-mile ski marathons, by small conventions. The family-oriented Christmas holiday package and the New Year's Eve package are sellouts. The Christmas week is arranged with special events: Christmas Eve religious services, Christmas Day cocktail party, Santa Claus with gifts for the children, entertainment programs for the children, Christmas dinner, movies, baby-sitting

CAGE FERRY

This amazing but short-lived cage ferry was devised by a lumber baron in the early 1900s to get supplies, animals, <u>and</u> men quickly across the river and into the camps. It ran suspended along cables stretched across the river.

for all adult events, dancing every night, plus special activities organized by the Social and Sports Director. The New Year's package includes all of this plus a New Year's Eve Gala dinner and, to keep the children busy while that is going on, a special New Year's Eve Children's Party.

Besides Chateau Montebello (which is open to the public for dining only if there is space left after the registered guests have dined), there are two other good places to eat in the area: the Pot au Feu on the main street in Montebello and the Crêperie de la Petite Ecole, situated on Papineau Street, one street north of Main Street. This delightful little red-and-white-frame restored schoolhouse is so like the one-room schoolhouse in which I taught at Beechgrove, Quebec, when I was only eighteen that I stood in shock when I first came upon it while out photographing in the area. La Petite Ecole specializes in fondues and 30 different kinds of crêpes.

SIDE TRIP NORTH UP HIGHWAY NO. 323

This side trip from Montebello leads to Val-Quesnel and St.-André-Avellin, through what is said to be some of "the most beautiful scenery" in an area of beautiful scenery. In the picturesque Québécois village of St.-André-Avellin, don't miss a stone church dating back to 1886 and the Boyer residence, a nineteenth-century brick with five unusual rounded dormers, each decorated with a carved finial.

Four blocks on is the artists' cooperative, L'Association coopérative des Artisans de la Vallée de la Petite Nation. A few miles further on is the L'Alandier de là Côte, the pottery shop of Diane Beauséjour-Aubry and Jean Aubry.

Carillon–Pointe Fortune Ferry

Travel east on Highway No. 148 from Montebello to Carillon, a multi-interest historic site involving the old Carillon Canal and Quebec Hydro's Carillon Dam. The Orgenteuil Historical Society Museum is housed in an old barracks.

The site embodies something for every member of the family —
a nature centre, a walking trail, tours of the dam by Quebec
Hydro, and a picnic park. Two miles upriver at the provincial
government park Dollard Désormeaux, there is another picnic
site, with boating facilities.

DIRECTIONS

After exploring Carillon, you can take the ferry to Pointe Fortune
(a summer ferry only) and pick up Highway No. 17 for the trip
home. Highway No. 417 offers you an alternate route back to Ottawa, and from this road, if you have the time, you can start the
tour of Glengarry County that is presented in the next chapter.

CHAPTER 2

GLENGARRY DAYS

Preamble

In Glengarry County the Scots have put down 200 years of history, and the imprint is so deep you can still travel back concession roads where every mailbox "down the line" will repeat the same clan name, McLeod, MacMillan, McGillivray, Cameron. In the "wilds" of Kenyon you can still hear Gaelic, the "language of the Garden of Eden," visit old houses that were not just a hundred or so years old — as in the rest of the Ottawa Valley — but bicentennial houses, and, at Maxville, annually attend the largest Highland Games in North America.

¶STORY

Lieutenant Colonel John Gillies told a story of the Michaud family, some of the strongmen of Glengarry who lived in the vicinity of Alexandria. John Michaud, as a young man, had killed a bear by choking it to death with his bare hands. All of John Michaud's sons were big, powerful men like their father, who was French Canadian but had married a Scot — an ethnic marital mix common in Glengarry.

A long time ago there was an American cattle buyer named

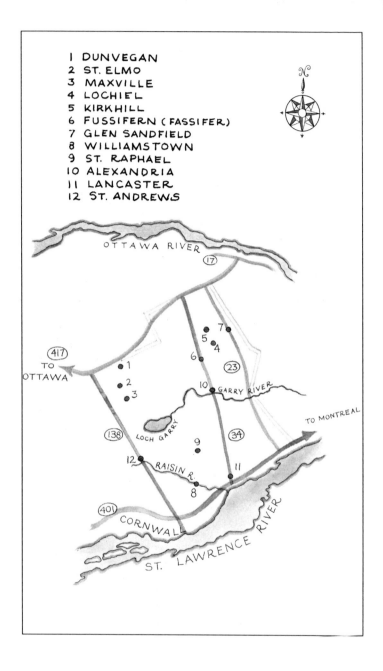

1 DUNVEGAN
2 ST. ELMO
3 MAXVILLE
4 LOCHIEL
5 KIRKHILL
6 FUSSIFERN (FASSIFER)
7 GLEN SANDFIELD
8 WILLIAMSTOWN
9 ST. RAPHAEL
10 ALEXANDRIA
11 LANCASTER
12 ST. ANDREWS

Latham who used to travel through Glengarry buying livestock, which he shipped to the American side. One day while travelling near Alexandria, Latham passed the Michaud farm. One of the sons was in the field near the road, clearing the land of stone and boulders. The cattle buyer stood and watched the ease with which young Michaud laboured with his heavy loads.

"What on earth can they grow on such rocky land?" the cattle buyer asked himself.

Curious, he got out of his buggy and approached young Michaud.

"What do you grow here?" he asked.

Young Michaud did not like Yankees, nor did he appreciate the slur on his father's land. He put down the big boulder he was lifting, straightened himself up very tall, and said: "What do we grow here, mister? We grow men here."

✳

I consider all of Glengarry County to be worth seeing, savouring, exploring, visiting. Therefore I am simply going to do the area town by town and site by site. Glengarry is a glory of exquisite little untouched towns like Summerstown and Williamstown, of truly sensitive and responsible restoration, and of heritage buildings, outstanding museums, and historic treasures. If you have time to dawdle with the old-timers, it is also profoundly rich in story and legend. The problem is that the Scots, unlike the Irish, only "open up" in their own sweet time.

HISTORY

Glengarry County once ran from the St. Lawrence River in the south to the Ottawa River in the north, but was reduced in size when Prescott County was carved out to the north. Writer Lauchlin MacInnes in his booklet *Glengarry and Western Gaelic* delineates "Greater Glengarry," which includes Cornwall, Finch, and Avonmore to the west, north into Prescott County, and east into Quebec, all originally spheres of Scottish settlement and influence. But today Glengarry County proper is smaller, running roughly from Dunvegan on the north, Maxville on the west, Glen Robertson and Glen Sandfield on the east. Five rivers run through

Glengarry: the Nation, Scotch, Beaudette, Raisin, and Garry. Glengarry fronts on the St. Lawrence.

The settlement of Glengarry in the eighteenth century was achieved by two groups of people: United Empire Loyalists from the United States and emigrants from the Scottish Highlands. Disbanded Loyalist soldiers and settlers who wished to remain loyal to the British Crown came north from the Mohawk Valley with Sir John Johnson when he fled the effects of the American Revolution. Having arrived at Cornwall (or "New Johnson," as it was then called in compliment to Sir John and to the capital of their former settlement in the fertile Mohawk Valley, Johnstown), the soldiers found the government land agent and forthwith proceeded to draw by lottery the lands that had been granted to them. Thus did men who had fought side by side in the ranks find themselves side by side working to clear and farm *tir nan coilltean mora* (the land of the great forests). This United Empire Loyalist influx began in 1778, peaked in 1784, and continued into 1789.

Then came the Highland immigrants expelled by the cruel Highland Clearances, which drove families from their homes in Scotland so that landlords could raise sheep. They came along the St. Lawrence River, led by Father Scotus Macdonell in 1786 and more Macdonells and their clan under Alexander Macdonell (Greenfield) in 1793. The ships' lists from those early years include MacLeods, McGillivrays, MacCuaigs, McIntoshes, Camerons, Macphersons, MacMillans, Kennedys, MacLeans, Grants, Camerons, MacPhees, MacKinnons. Perhaps more clannish in transplantation (the Scots of Glengarry to this day are accused of being "more Scottish than Scottish"), members of each clan settled side by side on the same concession, and to a certain extent the county remains in holdings that way today.

Dunvegan

To enter into this "Holy Land," you can take Highway No. 417 east toward Montreal and drop off at Highway No. 20, the Dunvegan–Maxville cutoff. Go east on No. 24 to Dunvegan, a charming historic little village in the north of Glengarry

County and near St. Elmo and Maxville, and the site of the Glengarry Pioneer Museum, one of the most gratifying museum complexes in the Ottawa Valley. Opened in 1962 to preserve and display artifacts from the days of pioneer Glengarry, the museum complex centres around a log inn dating from the settlement of Dunvegan about 1840. There is a log barn from a nearby farm as well as the livery shed from the township hall in Greenfield and a miniature cheese factory with authentic equipment. The 1867 Roxborough Township Hall from Warina has been relocated on the grounds as the Ivan Grant Buildings; with wonderful Scottish logic, it is furnished with displays relating to the history of local municipal government.

The log house began as McIntosh's Store, then became the Star Inn in the mid-1800s; it is furnished to the period with the original barrooms and bar still intact, a dumbstove, many pieces of fine old furniture, china, treen and several clocks, an important collection of early everyday clothing, and textiles, including work by the village weaver, John Dickson.

The centrepiece of the museum is a very large antique iron cooking pot out of which the Eight Outlaws of Glenmoriston fed Bonnie Prince Charlie when he was in hiding with them at Coiraghoth during his escape in 1746. The eight redoubtables were, more or less, Don Chisholm, his two brothers Hugh and Alex, a MacDougall, two Macdonalds, Hugh MacMillan, a MacPherson. The fabled pot, brought from Scotland in the immigration wave from Scotland in 1780-90, was treasured for years by the Chisholms. A present-day descendant of the Chisholms, Mickey MacDougall of Cornwall, gave the pot to Hugh MacMillan of the Ontario Archives for placement in the Dunvegan Museum.

The reason the Scots create such great museums is that they treasure their history. The Reference Room of Dunvegan Museum has an extensive collection of rare books, a score of Gaelic Bibles, the Book of Common Prayer in Hanks, the complete work of Ralph Connor and, a recent addition, the first registers of the Caledonia Springs Hotel, dating back to July 1845, when Lady Allen Napier MacNab and her daughter Sophia of Dundurn Castle in Hamilton breakfasted on champagne. The later guest lists reveal that the timber barons of the Upper Ottawa — the Whites of Pembroke and the O'Briens and Barnetts of Renfrew — had come for the sulphur spring cures. Picnic tables are available on the spacious shady grounds.

The Kenyon Presbyterian church in Dunvegan was in 1934 the scene of the last church service in Gaelic, ending 150 years of worship in the language of the Celts.

❡ STORY

There is an old Highland legend of "Bird Songs in Gaelic," the lovely and fanciful ancient belief about a long-ago and mystical time when even "the birds had the Gaelic" *A Bheil Gaidhlig agad?* (Is the Gaelic at you?)

✳

SIDE TRIP IN GLENGARRY

After Dunvegan you can wander around and explore the back townships of Glengarry — along Highway Nos. 21, 22, 24, and 30 for example — and visit Kenyon, Lochiel, Charlottenburg, with their untouched "service centres"; Kirkhill, Fussifern, and Glen Sandfield, where some of the farming land was so impoverished it was claimed that a young lad "could hop to school from stone to stone without ever touching the ground." This is the country of the legendary giant, Rory MacLennan, of whom 'twas said "he grew up on a farm so poor they lived on peas." Never mind. Out of these humble and difficult beginnings Glengarry County was to produce for Canada great explorers and fur traders, great educators and professionals, bankers, economists, and entrepreneurs. And Rory MacLennan's was a Horatio Alger story, proceeding from "pease porridge hot" to the lifestyle of a bachelor millionaire railway builder.

HISTORY

On May 24, 1877, six-foot-six Rory MacLennan, the Glengarry Giant, was giving a hammer-throwing exhibition for a large crowd attending the Victoria Day celebrations in Cornwall. One of the outstanding athletes of early Canada, MacLennan held the local record for the hammer throw. To protect the large crowds at the early Highland Games, officials had cordoned off an area with ropes. Unfortunately, however, just as MacLennan was winding up for a throw, a mother called her small daughter to her side and the child ran right into MacLennan's hammer. She was killed instantly. The young giant broke down and cried; he never threw the hammer again and withdrew from all athletics to become a major entrepreneur of the nineteenth century in Canada. Novelist Ralph Connor incorporated the tragedy into one of his books on early life in Glengarry County.

✠ STORY

Thomas McClelland of Dalkeith in Glengarry County had one night been very long in the hotel at Vankleek Hill. Now McClelland had been trying to learn to play the bagpipes but he was without very much talent. And he had been long in the hotel at Vankleek Hill while his cows had been bawling to be milked down in the pasture at the end of the lane. So McClelland decided he would soothe their savage breasts and pipe them into the cowbarn. He slipped into his house, took up his beloved bagpipes, and started piping himself in the dark down the lane to bring in his cows. But the wild caterwauling of the bagpipes in the dark of the night only terrified the poor cows so much that they stampeded and took off down the fields, and over the fences, and into the neighbour's crops. And it was morning before McClelland got them rounded up again and into the barn to be milked.

✳

Williamstown

Drive south down either Highway No. 34 or 20 to No. 18 and then to Williamstown, a village that might well be called "The Jewel of Glengarry." It is a veritable mecca of history-filled streets, astonishing mansions, the exceptional Nor'Westers and Loyalist Museum, and some of the oldest churches in Ontario. Williamstown was settled in 1784 by Sir John

Johnson and his Loyalist followers from Upper New York State. Many substantial and stately residences were subsequently built in and around this village by the United Empire Loyalists.

If, in the first years of the nineteenth century, Glengarry County was almost 100 percent Scottish, so was the roster of officers and partners in the fur-trading Nor'Westers Company at its inception in 1802: John Gregory, William McGillivray, Duncan MacGillivray, William Mallowell, Roderick Mackenzie, Angus Shaw, Daniel Mackenzie, William McKay, John Macdonald, Donald McTavish, Hugh McGillis, David Thompson, and Aeneas Cameron, to name a few. Many of the company leaders — Duncan Cameron, John MacGillivray, John Macdonald of Garth (Monsieur Macdonald le bras croche), Angus Macdonell (Greenfield), Alexander Macdonell (Greenfield), Hugh McGillis, and Astronomer Royal David Thompson — all retired to Glengarry after their fortunes were made and their fur-trading careers were over. This is the part of the logic for having the Nor'Westers and Loyalist Museum in Glengarry.

Again the Scots have shown their wisdom by lodging their history in an important building that should be preserved in this case, a huge, elegant Georgian 1862 school, a testimonial to how much money there was in those days in Williamstown, as well as a further substantiation of the importance the Scots always attached to education.

The museum features a huge map of all the North West Company trading posts and also all kinds of fascinating memorabilia and artifacts relating to the fur trade and the company business. On display is a wedding Bible that the famous explorer Sir Alexander Mackenzie, one of the directors of the North West Company, gave to his natural daughter, Maria, on August 22, 1825, the eve of her wedding. And here is recorded the story of Finnan "The Buffalo" Macdonald of Lot 3, Concession 2, Charlottenburg Township, Glengarry County.

HISTORY

In 1808 Finnan Macdonald went with explorer-surveyor David Thompson on a journey across the Rockies. Somewhere on the prairies, when the group was desperately in need of fresh meat, Macdonald volunteered to track a herd of buffalo. He shot but only wounded a young buffalo. Enraged, the bull charged Finnan and there followed a three-hour fight running on into the dark in which Finnan was gored countless times. Macdonald survived and returned to Glengarry as the legendary Finnan "The Buffalo."

Sir John Johnson's Manor House

Probably the oldest house in Ontario, still set in spacious grounds, Sir John Johnson's Manor House by several accounts dates back to 1784. The front door and flanking windows mark the original section of the rambling frame, which is today used as the town library. Despite Sir John's Anglo-American background, there is an undeniably French flare in the architecture of the Manor House, in the dormers and the steep pitch of the roof.

A French influence in Glengarry was quite logical: with the Quebec border only 60 miles away Glengarrians were bound to be commingling with, and influenced by, their French neighbours. But the traditional intermingling went deeper than that. If the directors of the North West Company were Scottish, the *voyageurs* and other employees, of whom there were hundreds, were principally French Canadians, and during the War of 1812 they formed that distinguished corps known as the Corps des Voyageurs Canadien. In Glengarry itself, amongst the farming Scots, particularly those close to the border, there were a number of Rousseaus, Gadbois, and Leroux, most of them shopkeepers and tradesmen in towns.

✦ STORY

It was perhaps the easy-come, easy-go fiddlin' fanciful Irish the entrepreneurial, education-oriented Glengarrians looked down upon, as evidenced by these two sayings gathered in the "Holy Land" recently:

The dumbest man in Kerry moved to Cork and, when he did that, the overall intelligence in both counties went up. The people of Cork claim they are the Paris of Ireland, but it is doubtful if the people of Paris feel they are the Cork of France.

✳

This extraordinary house was lived in by two extraordinary people: the Reverend John Bethune, first Presbyterian minister of Upper Canada and an ancestor of Dr. Norman Bethune, the Canadian physician honoured for his humanitarian work in China, and David Thompson, cartographer-explorer.

Tradition assigns a date of 1804–05 for the construction undertaken by Bethune, again showing strong French Canadian influence in the main buildings, in its gable roofs swept out over verandas in bell-cast curves, and in its stucco finish. On Bethune's death in 1815 Thompson, who had already explored and charted over 1.5 million square miles of Canadian wilderness, settled down with his wife and 13 children to try his hand at farming.

In 1977, recognizing the historical importance of the Bethune–Thompson House, the Ontario Heritage Foundation acquired it. In several years of archaeological diggings on the site, thousands of artifacts were uncovered, indicating the relative affluence of those who had lived here, as well as verifying that sections of the house had been built at different times over almost two centuries. The house, now operating as a museum, displays these archaeological artifacts, family papers, and early furnishings.

Fraserfield

In 1883 the authors of *Canadian Pen and Ink Sketches* remarked: "We had no idea that so grand a building was to be found in the wilds of Glengarry." Neither did I! Fraserfield, although still showing signs of wear and now in the process of restoration, is an astonishing discovery, coming as a complete shock amongst the modest farmhouses just west of Williamstown. But there it stands, a magnificent neo-classical mansion, commanding a sweeping prospect from a height of land, looking to the Adirondacks in the south, its classical proportions crowned by an imposing cupola.

Colonel Alexander Fraser's fortunes were largely the fruit of his talents in administration and politics. He apparently prospered as a quartermaster in Glengarry during the War of 1812. He was prominent as a colonel in the local militia; as a member of the Legislative Assembly of Upper Canada; as warden of the United counties of Stormont, Dundas, and Glengarry; and as local land titles registrar during the 1840s. Throughout Fraser's long political career, his "farm" of over 1,000 acres was very well managed, as was this house, with a formal walled garden surrounding it, standing at the junction of no less than three private, tree-lined entrance lanes, and always, in its early days, lavishly landscaped.

Begun soon after the War of 1812, Fraserfield is a fieldstone mansion, covered in stucco and scored to resemble an ashlar finish. The mansion's distinction lies in its sheer size and proportions, as well as in its exquisite detailing both outside and inside. Present owners George and Mary Lang and their seven children are restoring the house with the financial assistance of the Ontario Heritage Foundation.

McLean–Munro House

This house was built about 1810 when Cornwall was only a fledgling settlement. Through the years the large log house has been a well-known landmark, prized by history buffs as one of the four oldest and most significant buildings in that city. Patriarch Neil McLean had been sheriff in the district and a colonel at the Battle of Crysler's Farm during the War of 1812. He represented the area in provincial politics for years afterward. His son Archibald was MPP for several terms and a lawyer in Cornwall. In fact, many of Neil McLean's descendants became active in politics and influential in business, with close connections to many of the powerful institutions of the day, including the Family Compact, the military, and the Nor'Westers Company.

Therefore, it came as a shock to the Cornwall community when it was learned that the McLean house in 1961 was slated for demolition. The Stormont, Dundas, and Glengarry Historical Society rallied for its preservation but ultimately could effect only a compromise: it was agreed that the house would be dismantled, log by log, all the interior trim catalogued, and the material stored for a future rebuilding. Fourteen years later the Historical Society sold a pile of numbered logs, moldings, floorboards, doors, windows, and exceptional trim to Kitty and Stuart Munro on condition that the house be reconstructed within the bounds of the three counties. Just south of Williamstown, adjacent to the river amid a stand of old trees, the Munros found their site, where the McLean–Munro House now sits, in great pride, covered with blue clapboard, complete in every detail after four years of work. However, this was no ordinary log settler's house. The logs were hewn and dovetailed with precision and the house boasts other exterior sophistications, such as meticulous joinery, an oval gable window, and pilastered door cases with rare matching window cases. The fireplace mantels and the staircase are interior details that rival those of grander homes of the period.

St. Raphael's Church Ruins on the King's Road

Early in September 1786 a group of some 500 Jacobite Scottish Highlanders under the leadership of Father Scotus Macdonell emigrated from Knoydart, Scotland, to Glengarry County, Upper Canada. East of the present-day ruins they built one of the first churches in the country, the famous "Blue Church," which the Roman Catholics dedicated to the Archangel St. Raphael.

In 1815 construction on the replacement for the Blue Chapel was begun with stone carried from two district quarries by stone boat in the summer and by sleighs in the winter. Under the supervision of Bishop Alexander Macdonell and Archibald Fraser, a stonemason from Scotland, the church was built partly by subscription and partly by voluntary workers, some of them Protestant.

In August 1970 flames destroyed the interior of St. Raphael's, bringing to an end 150 years of continuous service. Rebuilding the church to its former size and grandeur seating 1,000 worshippers was out of the question for the remaining 150 families in the parish. In 1974 the Ontario Heritage Foundation agreed to stabilize the ruins of St. Raphael's. Today, along with its storied old graveyard, it has become one of the "shrines" of the Scottish Holy Land. Many early entries in St. Raphael's records are in Gaelic.

ꝰ STORY

Fifty-seven years ago Lieutenant Colonel John A. Gillies, one of the Gillies lumbering dynasty of Braeside, and himself a huge Scot, told a story that both illuminates earlier times in Glengarry and demonstrates the Scottish sense of humour:

In 1837 when the first church in the district — the Roman Catholic "Blue Church" at St. Raphael's — was built the Presbyterians had contributed quite liberally, feeling a certain debt because, prior to the erection of the first Presbyterian church

ST. RAPHAEL'S CHURCH RUINS

St. Raphael's Church was first built in the late 18th century by Jacobite Scottish Highlanders. The church burned in 1970, bringing to an end almost two centuries of worship on this site. The ruins have been stabilized and opened to the public.

at Martintown, a number of Protestant families had not hesitated to use the Catholic church for baptisms and marriages.

In the 1840s when the Presbyterians decided to build their own place of worship, recalling how they had helped out the Roman Catholics with their Blue Church, the building committee decided to let the Roman Catholics reciprocate the favour by helping them with their new church. Five members of the committee called on Father John MacDonald of St. Raphael's and asked for his help. Father John listened carefully.

"I am sorry, my friends," he said, "but the principles of my church will not permit me to help you build a Protestant church."

The committee was shocked and rose to leave but not before one of them reminded the priest how they had helped the Catholics with the Blue Church.

"Where are you building your new church?" the priest asked.

"On the site of the old one."

"Then you will have to tear down the old one first?"

The committee nodded in the affirmative.

"In that case I will donate £10 [$50] toward destroying the old church. That will be quite in keeping with my principles," laughed Father John.

Colonel Gillies reported that the contribution of $50 was paid out of the funds of St. Raphael's Church, and there stands to this day a record on the church books that reads: "the amount expended in demolishing Presbyterian church at Martintown, ten pounds."

✳

St. Andrew's Presbyterian Church

Again one of the oldest churches in Canada, *circa* 1812, this beautiful little stone church on a shady back street of Williamstown with its ancient, lumpy graveyard is a history lesson in itself. The Reverend John Bethune, as the first Presbyterian minister in Upper Canada, was also a leader in the struggling fledgling community. The parsonage, which he built (the Bethune–Thompson House) and where he and his wife Véronique raised a family of nine children, must have been a hive of social activity throughout Bethune's tenure.

In 1813 the daredevil leader, Lieutenant "Red George" Mac-donell led the Glengarry Highlanders and a few other troops across the ice on the St. Lawrence to storm and capture the fortified post at Ogdensburg. Perhaps part of their success was due to the fact that they were accompanied on either flank by two strange "bedfellows" — their two Gaelic-speaking chaplains, the Reverend Alexander Macdonell of St. Raphael's, later known as "The Big Bishop," and the Reverend John Bethune, founder of St. Andrew's. Once again the inevitable religious rivalry and ill will had been superseded by the clannishness of all Scots!

✻

Back in the days of Bishop Macdonell, a distinguished Scottish officer who had served in Canada for some years was visiting the bishop before returning home to Scotland. He told the priest that he would like to meet some of the veterans of the War of 1812 so that he might take their tales back home with him. The bishop took the soldier to see old John Roy, known as a great storyteller in Glengarry.

Now old John Roy had lived through many trials and effected many miraculous escapes, but he was most famous for taking charge of a large party of men, women, and children and bringing them safely through the wilderness from Schenectady, New York, to Glengarry County, Upper Canada.

"In Gaelic, with such an audience of illustrious and fascinated listeners, Roy omitted no details of that legendary journey: the number of men, women, and children he had brought with him; their perils and their escapes; how, when on the verge of starvation, they had boiled their moccasins and eaten them; how they had beaten back the wild beasts and the Indians.

"At the end of this spellbinding tale, the general said: 'Mr. Roy, the only journey I can compare this to is that of Moses leading the children of Israel to the Promised Land.'

"Up jumped old John Roy. 'Moses!' he cried out. 'Compare *me* to Moses! He lost half his army in the Red Sea! I brought my people through without losing a man!' "

✻

Special Events

If you are planning a visit to Williamstown, perhaps you might like to make it coincide with two of Glengarry's special events.

The *Williamstown Fair* takes place in early August on the fairgrounds behind the Nor'Wester and Loyalist Museum. Said to be the oldest fair in Ontario, it has been held annually since 1818.

The famous *Highland Games*, an annual event steeped in Scottish heritage, attracting as many as 26,000 people, takes place in nearby Maxville (on Highway No. 20) on the first Saturday in August. The Highland Games feature athletic contests, strongmen competitions, Highland dancing and music, bands, storytelling, sometimes in Gaelic. On the following Sunday a calarena is held at the ruins of St. Raphael's with games for children, more music and dancing, a chicken barbecue.

HISTORY

From the *Evening Citizen*, Ottawa, Friday, May 23, 1930:

ARE THERE ANY BIG SCOTSMEN LEFT?

"Are there any big powerful Scotsmen left in Glengarry, or Stormont, or Russell, or any of the surrounding counties?

The committee representing the Scottish Societies of Ottawa, for the Scottish games here on June 28, is thinking of offering a prize for the biggest Scotsman appearing on the grounds in his kilts.

The committee would also like to organize contests to ascertain if modern Scottish giants can uphold, equal, or surpass the records set by the old-timers."

The advertisement did not "come out of nowhere." The Scottish race in Canada, besides a number of other things, had contributed the majority of the legendary giants of the nineteenth-century, Angus McAskill of Cape Breton, the Twelve Macdonell Brothers of Sand Point (the shortest was six feet tall), The Last Laird MacNab of Arnprior, Rory MacLennan of Glengarry, Harry McLean of Merrickville.

✱

Cornwall

ollow the signs on Highway No. 401 to the Cornwall cutoff. Founded in 1784 by Scottish Loyalists from New York State, this town today has a large French-speaking population. It developed as an important religious and educational centre for Glengarry, Stormont, and Dundas counties. Construction of a canal between 1834 and 1842 provided improved transportation and water power for the numerous mills and textile plants located along the waterfront and thus contributed to Cornwall's industrial growth. The advent of the St. Lawrence Seaway resulted in the closing of the Cornwall Canal in 1953. The base of the swing bridge survives.

WALKING TOUR

A walking tour of centretown Cornwall includes:

• The old *Capital Theatre* (29 Second St. West), now protected under the Ontario Heritage Foundation Act.

• *Trinity Anglican Church* (105 Second St. West), an 1869 memorial to Bishop John Strachan, has the earliest tombstone in the adjacent cemetery, dating back to 1789.

• The *Baily–John Sandfield MacDonald House* (40 York St.) *circa* 1851, was lived in by John Sandfield Macdonald, first premier of Ontario, and later by Dr. Charles Rattray, prominent physician and mayor of Cornwall.

• The *Stormont Row Housing* (York St.) was industrial row housing erected in 1881 for the employees of the Stormont Cotton Mill.

• *John Chesley's Inn* (40 First St. West) was built in Georgian style in the 1820s for one of Cornwall's prominent leaders. It has been converted to a residence.

• The *Cornwall Canal*, stretching 11 1/2 miles from Cornwall to Dickinson's Landing, was built to bypass the Long Sault Rapids.

• The *Superintendent's Residence* is a handsome large brick built in 1872 for superintendents of the canal. Superintendents were responsible for the upgrading, maintenance, and efficient operation of the canal and its series of locks. The building is now headquarters local RCAF.

• The *District Courthouse and Gaol* (7 Water St. West), at age 150, is one of the oldest remaining public structures in Ontario. It replaced earlier older buildings dating back to the 1793, when Cornwall was first designated a site for the courthouse.

• *Bojangles* (58-62 Pitt St.) and *Joe the Tailor* (9 First St. East) are fine examples of early commercial architecture.

• The *Andrew Hodge House* (125 First St. East) was built by prominent mill owner Andrew Hodge around 1860.

• The *Cline House* (203 Second St. East) was built in 1854 shortly after the marriage of Samuel Cline to Margaret Dickinson. The house remained with the Cline family until 1955, when it became the Cornwall Public Library.

• *Knox–St. Paul's United Church* (108 Second Ave. East) was built in 1895, designed by the noted Toronto firm of Gordon and Helliwell.

• The *House of Labour* (130 Sydney St.), a Gothic Revival Baptist church, was erected in 1884. It is now a meeting hall.

• The *United Counties Museum* (731 Second St. West) is located in the Hood House.

Inverarden Regency Cottage Museum

Located at the junction of Boundary Road and Montreal Road (Highway No. 2) is the Inverarden Regency Cottage Museum, *circa* 1825. The Glengarrians score again with this truly outstanding museum. As they did with the Dunvegan Museum (an early stopping-place) and the Nor'Westers and Loyalist Museum (an old school), they have assured the survival of this rare building by making it into a museum.

Inverarden, "the high headland where the river meets the sea," was built in 1816 for retiring North West Company fur-trading partner, John Macdonald of Garth. It is now the finest remaining example of Regency Cottage architecture in Ontario.

After a year and a half in Montreal spending a goodly portion of his 11,000-pound fortune "amidst gaiety, amusements, and feasting," at age 45, Macdonald brought his family to Cornwall. Within a decade he had over 60 tenants living and working at Inverarden, or "Gart," as he called it.

INVERARDEN REGENCY COTTAGE MUSEUM

This regency-style cottage was built for retiring North West Company fur-trader John MacDonald in 1816. The museum offers a guided tour, a local history slide presentation, and an extensive library of rare books.

The museum offers a guided tour of the house and its nine rooms, refurnished in Regency period (some of the furniture original to the owners), as well as a local history slide presentation, lectures on early Canadiana, travelling art and photography exhibitions, musical soirées, and craft shows.

The museum library has rare books and tapes for reference and study. A museum gift shop features the work of local artisans and items of local historic interest.

Pioneer Corner Craft Co-op

On Highway No. 2, four kilometres west of Cornwall and 30 kilometres east of Upper Canada Village, is the Pioneer Corner Co-op. Pioneer Corner began in Centennial year 1967, when Stanley McNairn moved two log houses to their present location, where for 14 years a variety of local crafts and foods were sold. In 1981 20 local craftsmen formed a cooperative to buy the log buildings and sell their handicrafts, collectibles, and consignment items from local people.

Alexandria

Priest's Mill Restaurant and Pub in the old town of Alexandria (at the junction of Highway Nos. 34 and 10), betimes known as the "Hub of Glengarry," is one of the finest heritage dining places not only in the county but in the whole province of Ontario.

The first Priest's Mill was built on the Garry River in 1819 by the Reverend Alexander Macdonell to meet the needs of the parishioners of St. Raphael's. Alexandria was originally named Priest's Mills for the number of mills that sprang up there; as early as 1823 there were 12 buildings on the site.

The Grand Trunk Railway passed through Alexandria, and by 1900 the town had developed a number of industries, including the Munro and MacIntosh plant, which made the famous "Buggy from Glengarry." In 1848 the first wooden mill was destroyed by fire and replaced that same year by a stone one.

In 1942 the first restaurant was built on an old foundation adjacent to the mill. Glengarrians Mr. and Mrs. Evan McDonald bought the site in 1969, opened their first restaurant, and have been in a continuous process of careful restoration ever since. Recently, with the restaurant area finished, they have turned their preservation talents to the old stone store next door, where they have opened the Jenny William Store, featuring country and traditional gifts and decorating items, specializing in imported French lace, pine antiques, country dishes, and folk art.

The main dining room of Priest's Mill at the back looks out over the Garry River, the mill run, walled gardens. The site alone is worth a visit.

Alexandria is a charming Glengarry town, full of historic buildings not yet researched and catalogued. Across the street from the Priest's Mill is one of the few bookstores in the county specializing in local history, the Glengarry Bookstore.

Lancaster

For another Glengarry dining place, head to Lancaster, off Highway No. 401. The Lancaster Inn is huge and rambling, without any great decor or character, but it specializes in Lancaster perch and other fresh fish. (The perch was so good I went back again!) Outside the dining room windows, overlooking the St. Lawrence River, a huge cairn hulks against the skyline a little offshore. This Scottish monument was built in 1887 by the Glengarry Militia under Colonel Alexander Fraser of Fraserfield. That winter the Glengarry soldiers were hard pressed to find something to do and were getting "into trouble" in the town. So Lieutenant Colonel Lewis Carmichael put them to work building this monument, the largest cairn of its type in North America. Boat trips to the cairn can be arranged from the Lancaster Inn or its marina.

On December 9, 1872, Hamilton B. Wilson in the Old Country sent this letter to Andrew Harkness in Glengarry.

"Dear Sir:

I have this day seen a strong box packed and addressed to you. It contains your uncle's writing desk and inside the desk his watch and chain also his riding whip for your brother Robert. The box has painted on it the words 'Andrew Harkness Esq. M.D.C.K. Lancaster, Ontario, Canada.' I hope it will reach you in safety. It is being sent off this day to Derry by the train then it will go to Liverpool, and leave Liverpool on the 19th of this month by the ship 'Austrian' belonging to the line of Mesrs 'Allan Brothers & Co.', and will sail for Portland on your side of the water.

Mr. Dunbar has managed all this for you and has done so with the utmost readiness and goodwill.

> Believe me
> sincerely yours
>
> Hamilton B. Wilson"

The strongbox — and the letter! — to this day are with the Harkness family; indeed, with a fourth-generation Andrew Harkness!

Such pride of clan, ancestry, genealogy, such treasuring of family memorabilia is, in large part, responsible for the rich museums, the preservation of artifacts, the restoration of buildings in Glengarry.

DIRECTIONS

There are several ways to return to Ottawa. You can take Highway No. 401 East to No. 34 and head north until you come to No. 417, then head west to the Capital City. Or, with a good map in hand, you can wend your way back along the backroads and byways of Glengarry.

Chapter 3

THROUGH
LOVELY LANARK

Preamble

The Ottawa Valley was settled predominantly by the Irish, but the Scots put their stamp on two areas that they still regard as "Holy Land" — Glengarry County and Lanark County. Your lazy, gentle meanders through Lovely Lanark are trips for which I must warn you to fill your gas tank. Even today I usually get lost in Lanark — subconsciously I may do this on purpose so that I can see more of it.

First Tour

Balderson

To start your first one-day tour of Lanark County, get yourselves to Perth by whatever route is the fastest for you (Highway No. 7 out of Ottawa is one direct route; No. 10 is another.) Just west of

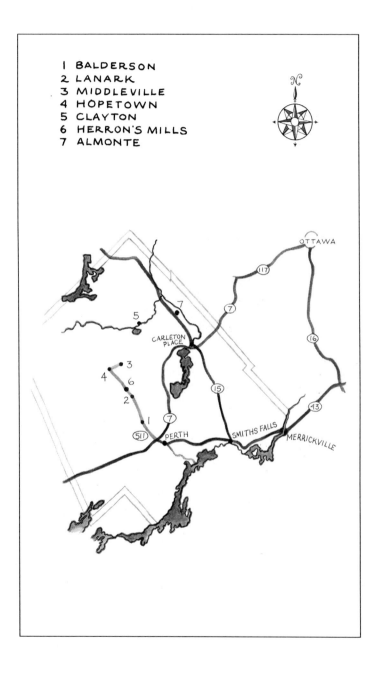

1 BALDERSON
2 LANARK
3 MIDDLEVILLE
4 HOPETOWN
5 CLAYTON
6 HERRON'S MILLS
7 ALMONTE

N

OTTAWA
117
7
16
CLAYTON 5
7 ALMONTE
CARLETON PLACE
3 MIDDLEVILLE
6 HERRON'S MILLS
4 HOPETOWN
2 LANARK
15
1 BALDERSON
7
43
511
PERTH
SMITHS FALLS
MERRICKVILLE

the stoplights on Highway No. 7, at Perth, turn north on No. 511 and head for Balderson. The Balderson Cheese Factory has been making award-winning cheese for 100 years now and recently replaced its old factory with a new building. If you make previous arrangements, you can have a tour. In any case, see the works, sample the ice cream and sandwiches, and taste the second-best Cheddar in Canada.

Lanark

Proceed along Highway No. 511 to the old town of Lanark, the spiritual heart of Lanark County. St. Paul's Anglican Church with its ancient tombstones is one of the most photogenic in the Valley. It was built in 1842, on land donated by an Irishman, James Monahan. Walk around Lanark, visit the woollen mill outlet there, the wool store next door, and the House of Five Shoppes across the street. Drop in for tea and homemade goodies at the Old Bank Restaurant and Bakery.

❡ STORY

Here's one from Lanark County:

There was an old fellow by the name of Paddy Vaughan in Carleton Place. He was a blacksmith. There was a fellow came in there one day to his blacksmith's shop and was boasting about how far back he remembered. Paddy listened for a while and then he said: 'Oh hell! I can remember back to the time in Carleton Place when the Mississippi River only ran as far as the bridge on Main Street.' "

✳

Herron's Mills

A few miles out of Lanark on No. 511, you'll come to a right turn in the road that leads into Herron's Mills, where James Gillies began his lumbering dynasty. The present owners are opposed to trespassers, but if you drive slowly you can see everything in this heritage complex of buildings. Then turn back and head north along Highway No. 511 to Middleville.

Middleville

This village looks and feels as though nothing had happened here for a hundred years. Actually, Middleville is steeped in history. Stop your car under a shady tree (one thing the town has lots of) and wander over to Trinity United Church. Here the late Mrs. D.A. Gillies of the Arnprior timber dynasty set into an upright encasement the tombstones of the earliest settlers in the area: the Lauries, Andersons, Baxters, Mathers, Borrowmans, Mackays, Crightons, Rankins, as well as Gillies, of course.

Kitty-corner from the Gillies monument is Danny Greer's General Store. It is no ordinary general store but special in two ways: although the new building is only 50 years old, Mr. Greer has kept all the old counters, fixtures, window seats, and benches from the original store. On these benches and window seats, as they have done for a hundred years in Lanark County, the "old lads" gather to forecast the weather, estimate the crops, tell tall tales, and reminisce about the great old times. Along with Lynch's General Store at McDougal, this is the last place I know of in the Valley where the "old lads" still gather.

The old stone schoolhouse is now Middleville Museum. It's usually open Saturday, Sunday, Monday, and Wednesday.

Middleville is famous for its Pioneer Days, which used to be held in August and attended by thousands of people from all over the Ottawa Valley. But the people who organized and ran the show have decided to take a rest for a few years.

Hopetown

From Middleville, go north on Highway No. 511 to Hopetown, once a thriving mill village on the Clyde. Robert Cannon was the first settler here in 1820, followed by the Bairds, Wilsons, Cummingses, McInneses, Moores, Murphys, Dobbies, Horns, and Stewarts. Duncan Stewart's tombstone in the Hopetown cemetery has one of those hauntingly disturbing verses:

"Hark from the tomb a doleful sound,
Mine ears attend the cry,
Ye living men must view the ground
Where you must shortly lie."

JAMES GILLIES HOUSE, HERRON'S MILLS

Built in 1861, the Gillies House at Herron's Mills is part of a unique heritage site including log barns, shanties, and mills set on 400 acres of land along the Clyde River.

Clayton

If you are adventurous, go north on Highway No. 511 to No. 9, turn east, and follow it into Clayton. Situated on the small but mighty Indian River, Clayton is one of the loveliest of the lovely towns of Lanark. Edmund Bellamy, a Vermonter, came up here in 1795 and built his first sawmill, which may account for the American influence on the architecture. McNeils, Bolgers, Bolands, Bannings, Raths, McMunns, and Blairs followed and built many of the town's fine colonial-style houses, many of which are restored now or in the process.

This is the place to picnic and swim. The townsfolk have made a beautiful little park close to Bellamy's Falls with tables under the willow trees and the water turbines and hasher plates preserved from the mill. Swimming in the falls is discouraged, but the town has a fine beach just a few yards away. Visit Gemmill's General Store, one of the great country stores in the Valley.

The Mill of Kintail

Sometime in the afternoon, if you can tear yourself away from Clayton, continue on Highway No. 9 to its junction with No. 11. Follow No. 16 east toward Almonte to the Mill of Kintail.

An imposing 1830 stone mill first named after its builder, Baird, and then renamed by its new owner after his ancestral home in Scotland, the Mill of Kintail is an extraordinary heritage site. Not only is it an exceptional pioneer mill, but it later became the summer home of Almonte's most famous native, Dr. R. Tait McKenzie, surgeon, world-famous pioneer in physical education for the disabled (deaf, blind, handicapped), and sculptor — one of a long procession of unrecognized Canadians.

A graduate of Lisgar Collegiate in Ottawa and McGill University, McKenzie went on to become Professor of Physical Therapy and Director of Physical Education at the University of Pennsylvania in Philadelphia. There, when lecturing in anatomy, instead of making flat blackboard drawings, he modelled his famous "Four Masks of Expression," showing the involuntary effects of stress on the athlete during various stages. Two of his hundreds of sculptures are the War Memorial "Home-coming at Cambridge, England" and "The Call," in Princess Street Gardens, Edinburgh, Scotland.

MIDDLEVILLE PIONEER CEMETERY

*Preserved in this wall beside Trinity United Church in Middleville
are the tombstones of the earliest settlers in the area.*

Major and Mrs. James F. Leys spent two years restoring the mill, which had fallen into ruin after McKenzie's death in 1939. Finally, in 1972, the Mississippi Valley Conservation Authority acquired the property, and the mill is now a museum housing McKenzie's athletic and memorial sculptures as well as early settlers' effects that he and others collected.

Some 130 acres have been added to the original hallowed ground of the Mill of Kintail property and the two miles of unspoiled walking trails are used by nature-study groups along both sides of the Indian River. Picnicking is allowed but no swimming.

Almonte

At Almonte, it's time for tea at the Waterford Tea Room in the Heritage Mall across from Rosamund's five-storey stone mill and within sound of the rush of Canada's Mississippi River. Real china and tablecloths, local paintings on the walls, all food homemade, Waterford is a rare cooperative: all the baked goods — bread, Black Forest cake, fresh rhubarb pie, wild strawberry shortcake, and fresh fruit flan — are made and brought in by local women. Owner Pamela Murphy does all the specials at home and delivers them to the tea room. On my day it was mouth-watering Scallops Waterford.

Waterford Tea Room does a heavy take-out business. If you get there before four o'clock, they will pack you a delicious picnic supper, which you can then take to the town park, a few hundred yards away, and dine on one of the picnic tables, eating of the best, and sprayed by the Mississippi falls and rapids.

You should also try to visit the Dalai Lama's Bakery. Among other things, it makes the best stone-ground whole-wheat raisin bread in North America. Stock up on some and head home for the freezer.

¶ S T O R Y

Dinny O'Brien of the Burnt Lands of Huntley, dead these forty years, was one of the great original wits of the Ottawa Valley.

Dinny O'Brien had great whiskers and in the wintertime these whiskers grew icicles, as did the whiskers of all the other whiskered gentlemen of Almonte. One cold, cold January day, very frosty, Dinny was in the Almonte Hotel. He had had a couple of drinks in the bar and was standing in the hotel lobby. The hotel was always badly heated, but Dinny had been in the bar long enough and had had fumes of alcohol strong enough to melt the icicles on his beard. Suddenly he looked up and saw this whiskered man coming down the stairs with a great crop of icicles on his beard.

" 'Well, well,' said Dinny, 'and what room did you sleep in?' "

✳

Second Tour

Proud Perth

The second one-day tour of Lanark includes Perth and Merrickville. Perth is fast becoming the Williamsburg of Canada. From Ottawa, head out to Bells Corners and take Highway No. 10 to Richmond, a charming and historic military settlement famous for its bakery. Since it expanded, the quality has gone down somewhat but it is still worth a stop to sample its "nearly" homemade bread.

The road from Richmond through Prospect was built to move troops in case of American attack. It is straight as a die except for a couple of 90-degree corners where the farmer wouldn't let the surveyors go through his fields. Hopefully, you won't be tempted to go so fast that you will miss some of the most well-preserved complexes of log buildings in the whole Valley. Follow No. 10 to its junction with Highway No. 15, go through Franktown, and pick up No. 10 again and proceed into beautiful Perth-on-the-Tay.

WALKING TOUR

Perthites are dedicated to preserving their heritage town and making people aware of Perth handicrafts. Walking tours of the town start from City Hall on the main street and also from the Big Cheese headquarters on Highway No. 7.

Abandon your car in a shady spot and walk the streets of Perth. Enjoy row after row of attractively restored houses through many tree-lined streets; be sure to look for such major landmarks as the Perth jail and courthouse. The Last Laird MacNab's settlers once walked from Arnprior along the Old Perth Road to an earlier courthouse on the same site to answer charges and suits brought against them by MacNab, their tyrannical "feudal" laird who rode through the bush trail on horseback.

You will see the arrogant 1830 house of Daniel McMartin, lawyer for MacNab, a formidable autocrat who "never allowed a client to sit in his presence" and who brought all the materials for his rare neo-classical mansion from the United States — probably one of the earliest recorded cases of the Canadian attitude that "nothing Canadian is good enough." When you come to John Haggart's great stone, hip-roofed Regency house you will quickly realize that the Haggarts were stonemasons before they became politicians and members of Parliament.

The exquisite colonial Georgian gem Inge-Va ("Come Here" in the Tamil language of Sri Lanka) was built in 1823 by a monied Irish cleric, the Reverend Michael Harris, and was later purchased by Thomas Radenhurst, Perth's second lawyer and counsel against McMartin for the settlers of Last Laird MacNab. The house is now cherished by Mrs. Charles Inderwick; upon her death, all its priceless treasures as well as the house itself will become a museum.

¶ STORY

This was told to me by a lady in Perth:

I hadn't really been out of Perth until I was 21, when my mother took me on the Grand Tour. She had been taken when she was 21 and so had her sister. It was pretty dull, in a way, but on the way home I fell in love and became engaged. I think for a long time I believed that you only fall in love once. For a long time I was a happy old maid: I had a good time; I had my own money. I fell heir to a 400-acre farm up on Dalhousie Lake and in 1939, for $10, I had a log house taken down, all the logs numbered and moved, and rebuilt it on the farm.

"The log house in 1939 was about 80 years old and it had a story. It was built by Pat and Mary Ryan, brother and sister. They had a house-raising bee when they built it. They all came and brought food and there was a barrel of whisky, but the women said, 'No

DANIEL MCMARTIN HOUSE, PERTH

This rare neo-classical mansion was built in 1830 by Daniel McMartin, lawyer for the Last Laird McNab. Materials for the house were imported from the United States.

whisky until the job is done.' They used to slide the logs up into place on skids and, of course, they got nibbling at the barrel and one fell and hit a man, injuring him seriously. But someone said, 'Never mind. It's just one of those Irishmen. There'll be another out in a week.' "

＊

HISTORY

Long ago, Perth was the scene of a most romantic episode. The last duel in Canada was reportedly fought there over a lady's honour — the beautiful Elizabeth Hughes, governess to the children of James Boulton, Perth's first lawyer. He built The Summit, one of the earliest brick houses in Ontario, around 1822, still in existence, and an exact replica of The Grange behind the Art Gallery of Ontario in Toronto. (Obviously, the members of the Family Compact influenced each other in more ways than one.)

Two young Perth law students, Henry Wilson and Robert Lyon, accompanied by their seconds, confronted each other with pistols by the banks of the Tay on the evening of June 13 in 1833. John Wilson, aged 23, killed Robert Lyon, aged 19. Wilson later married Miss Hughes and became an honoured lawyer and judge in St. Thomas, Ontario, where he built the fortress house Elmhurst.

It is said that forever afterward on the anniversary of the fatal duel, Wilson locked himself in his room and spoke to no one.

If the story of the Last Fatal Duel intrigues you, you can follow it to Matheson House Museum on the main street, where the pistols used in that encounter are displayed in a glass case. Down by the river, in the Old Burying Ground, you can still find the little tombstone of Robert Lyon.

Matheson House Museum is a cool refuge where there is displayed, among other things, the John Wilson collection of rocks, renowned amongst North American geologists. Wilson discovered both *Wilsonite* and *Perthite*, examples of which are in the cases.

Other Pleasures of Perth

Apart from all the history, Perth offers a great deal more for the day tripper. Two ideal swimming areas — the beach at Last Duel Park and supervised swimming in Stewart Park, which is also a picnic area — a homemade candy shop, an ice cream parlour, antique shops, an art gallery, a lovely bookstore to browse in and pick up your local histories: *Perth Remembered* edited by Edward Shortt, *The Memorable Duel at Perth* by the same writer, and *The Caldwells of Lanark* by E.L. Jamieson.

The River Guild, the largest cooperative outlet for craftsmen in the area, has a display of 18 local artisans and an apothecary shop specializing in rare and imported concoctions. It operates under the enticing slogan, "Only fools and flutterpates do not seek reverently for what is charming." Almost without exception, these commercial enterprises in Perth are now housed in restored heritage buildings. Shaw's Store is probably one of the oldest "department" stores in Ontario; your children should see it even if you buy nothing there.

If you haven't brought a picnic lunch — and maybe supper, too — Perth provides dining. The majority of restaurants can be found in the heart of town, on Gore or Drummond Street. For high tea with all the trimmings fine china and homemade treats visit the Blue Willow Tea Room. Charming. If you want drinks, Humdrum's patio overhanging the Tay is incomparable. Other possibilities worth investigating are: Maximillian's at the Hotel Perth; the Rideau Ferry Inn (that's down the road a bit but it's the great old dancing place of yesterday, now back in business with a vengeance); Patterson's Fine Dining on Highway No. 7; and Noonan's in the heart of town.

Famous for its schnitzel, Maximillian's offers dining with a strong Austrian influence. Patterson's is more formal and colonial than Noonan's, although both provide interesting ambiance. Humdrum's, an old stone structure embellished with good local paintings and photographs.

❡ STORY

This story came from an open-line radio program:

Mick Burns of Perth was one of the great characters of Lanark County. He was a great, great lad and a Roman Catholic. Now, one time the Presbyterian Church in Perth had a fire, a bad fire, and they wanted to hire someone to take the remains down and level it off. They asked Mick Burns what he'd charge for the job and he said, 'I'll take that damn Presbyterian thing down for nothing.' "

Merrickville

If you fall in love with Perth you'll want to take the loop home along Highway No. 43 and visit Merrickville, a small stone version of Perth, considerably restored and a dormitory town for Ottawa. This highway takes you through Smiths Falls and you should take time out to see one of the sights there. Just off the Old Sly Road, near the bridge and the new curling rink, you can see the heritage house that the women of Smiths Falls have been restoring. They claim it is the only house left in North America (it may have been the only one to begin with!) with a two-storey backhouse attached to an outside wall.

Continue on to Merrickville, originally Merrick's Mills — named after millwright William Merrick, the town's first settler who arrived in 1794. With the building of the Rideau Canal the village became a canal town and remains so today. The many and varied pleasure craft passing through it along the Rideau Waterway add to its innate charm.

Engineering genius and Valley giant Harry McLean made this town his base of operations for many years before his death in 1961. Deek's quarry outside of town was the supply centre for materials for his building projects. The huge stone four-storey "canal" building at the junction of the main streets (known as the McLean Block and now housing fashionable boutiques and the Copper Kettle, the town meeting and eating place) was his office, gymnasium, and guest quarters. His palatial stone house on Main Street, past the ancient Hotel Louis (which is supposed to have subterranean tunnels that allowed bootleggers and rumrunners from the Rideau Canal to move their cargo undetected), is now a Roman Catholic retreat for nuns — a sharp contrast from the days when McLean was entertaining the Glengarry Highland Games Pipe Band with cases of Johnny Walker, or hoisting a horse up the beautiful broad, winding staircase of the mansion as entertainment for guests from Chapleau and Minnesota.

The Block House Museum

The Block House Museum in Merrickville was built originally as a fort to protect the Rideau Canal from attack by Americans. The fort comes complete with moat and drawbridge. The museum is open daily. Guided walking tours of the village start from that point on Sundays.

In his later years, his dams and railways and aqueducts all built, Harry McLean returned to live in his favourite place — Merrickville, Ontario. Generally, the town was divided into two camps: those who enjoyed his madcap antics and eccentricities and opened their doors to his night prowlings, and those who regarded him as a form of outlandish outlawry and locked their doors upon him. A handful of people knew his abilities and his real generosity. A former resident of Merrickville told this one:

I'm not as old as Mr. McLean, but my dad was growing up in Merricville and was a teenager when H.F. was in his prime there. My uncle, my cousin, my dad, and myself were swimming at the fairgrounds outside of Merrickville when H.F. came down with his pilot to get into his seaplane to have a little fly around the country. He had with him his pet cat — a bobcat or a lynx or something like that. And he had this cat under one arm, and between taking swigs himself and trying to get the cat a little bit intoxicated, the cat had managed to claw him completely. He was blood from head to toe.

"We looked around for a place to go. My dad and my uncle hauled my cousin and myself out into the water, as this was the only place they figured we could all be safe from McLean. Yes, all the stories about his drinking capacity, they seem to be 100 percent true.

"McLean seemed to have a very close rapport with the children of Merrickville. Or so my dad tells me. I think the only people who didn't like him were the ladies of the town because they were afraid that their husbands were going to get too closely involved with him. I remember my dad telling me that he and his brother had done something one time for Mr. McLean, something quite inconsequential, and he gave them each $100. Dad still rues the day that he went home and told my grandmother that Mr. McLean had given them this big sum of money. Why? Because my grandmother promptly grabbed them both by the ears and marched them across town and made them give it all back."

*

SIDE TRIP UP HIGHWAY NO. 10

Just as all roads lead to Perth, so all roads lead from Perth. If you have time on your hands, want to see more of the countryside, and fancy yourself a hot-shot driver, take Highway No. 10, the Westport Road. It is one of the last untouched rally roads in Ontario — a paved, narrow, roller-coaster route that will delight your children as you maneuver the 90-degree turns. One place along the way is aptly called "Ups and Downs."

DIRECTIONS

For a scenic treat going home, swing onto Highway No. 36, pass through Crow Lake to Sharbot Lake on No. 38. From there, continue north to No. 7, which leads straight into the Queensway and home.

Chapter 4

AYLMER: THE LEISURE CAPITAL WITHIN THE CAPITAL

Preamble

The privileged geographical position of Aylmer is unquestionably one of its most appealing characteristics, located as it is in the heart of the National Capital Region, on the North Shore of the Ottawa River. From its centre the beautiful Eardley Road pushes upriver toward the Pontiac, and to its north stretch the priceless recreational resources of the Gatineau Park and the lovely lakes of the Gatineau Hills. Not for nothing has Aylmer been called "the Leisure Capital within the Capital."

Aylmer is endowed with five golf courses, all within touching distance of each other along the Aylmer Road: the Champlain, the Gatineau, the Chaudière, the Kingsway, the Rivermead, and the Royal Ottawa golf clubs. Interspersed amongst all these rolling greens is the renowned Connaught Jockey Club and racetrack and many of the "old stones" of Aylmer.

As if that were not enough to render the town exceptional in all the National Capital Region, Aylmer is also the site of one of the

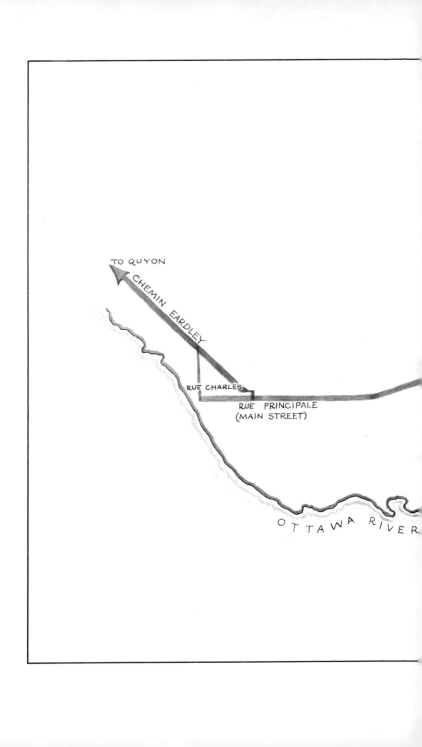

TO QUYON

CHEMIN EARDLEY

RUE CHARLES

RUE PRINCIPALE
(MAIN STREET)

OTTAWA RIVER

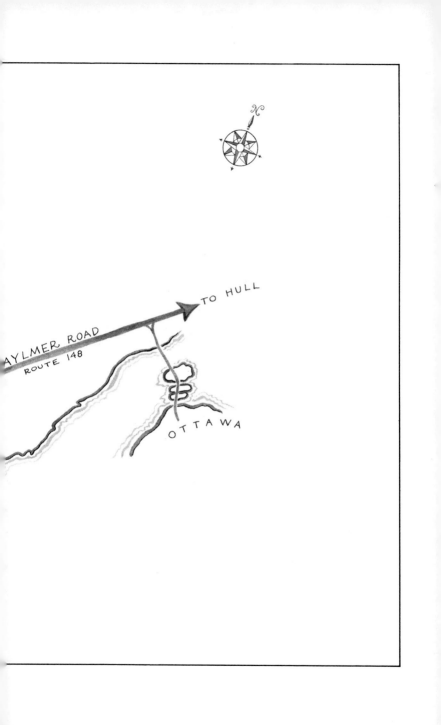

outstanding yacht clubs in the Valley. As well, it is endowed with little parks, a lengthy riverside bicycle and walking trail, and a warm "village" atmosphere, which alone makes it most desirable as a place to live — and a delightful place to visit.

Of all the areas sheltered under "the Greater Ottawa" umbrella, Aylmer is outstanding as a repository of our Canadian heritage. To a large extent, the old part of the town remains to this day nineteenth-century, manifesting its gentry and microcosmically embodying the history of the Ottawa Valley. Aylmer's Three Miles of History stretch from the Aylmer Road at the Champlain Bridge to the Landing Place at Symmes Inn and the Aylmer Marina on the Ottawa River.

Most of the storied residential areas of old Centretown and Lower Town in the capital have been virtually wiped out by the Greber Plan. And almost all of the great municipal buildings of Hull — the post office, the courthouse, the city hall, the old fire hall and police station, as well as whole streets of houses — were demolished to make way for the anonymous government buildings now high-rising against the Ottawa River skyline, replacing the many buildings that once gave Hull its distinctive Québécois character.

The Aylmer Road

B ack in the 1930s when I was a child growing up in Centretown, my family was one of the lucky ones on the block that always had a car usually a new one each year. In that unbearable season between skating and swimming — sometimes called spring — after Sunday school and church on Sunday, my father and mother would often try to alleviate our impatience with the winter that would never end and the summer that would never come. This was done by following a social custom of the time: packing us into the car and taking us for "the Sunday drive." This leisurely 20-mile-an-hour outing almost always took place along the Aylmer Road, where we ogled the stately mansions of the rich, the Sopers and the Eddys, and the house where Hollywood actress Maureen O'Hara was supposed to live. And then through Aylmer out onto the Eardley Road up the Pontiac, with my mother telling tales of some of the grand houses over-looking the river outside Aylmer.

A relative told me these bits and pieces of local lore:

In this house lived the McLeans. They were so tight they sat up all night picking the mustard seed out of their oats so they could get more money for it.

"Here lived the ——. They were so mean they wouldn't give old Doc Church permission on his winter house calls to go through their fields and avoid the great riverside snowdrifts.

"In this house lived the famous Doc himself. He invented his own snowmobile long before Bombardier and Ski-doo . . . necessity being the mother of invention."

*

DIRECTIONS

You can take the Queensway to Island Park Drive, still one of the most prestigious addresses in the capital. Follow Island Park due north until it becomes the Champlain Bridge crossing the mighty Ottawa River to the Quebec side.

Once over the bridge, follow your nose north (through the NCC tulips if it's spring) a short distance to a T with overhead stop-lights. Turn left, following the highway sign that points to Fort Coulonge. You will then be on the Aylmer Road, which eventually leads into Highway No. 148, going north from Aylmer to Sheenboro. For three miles the Aylmer Road remains, along with the Richmond Road south of Ottawa, one of the most historically rich routes in the whole Ottawa Valley. Perhaps finally realizing the singular heritage resources of Aylmer, along with municipal and heritage bodies, the Quebec government is now providing impetus and funds for the preservation of Aylmer, paradoxically an "English" town originally.

The early history of Aylmer springs directly out of the early history of Hull. In 1800 Philemon Wright and a handful of friends arrived from Massachusetts and, at the foot of the Chaudière Falls on the Ottawa River, began a settlement called Hull. In 1802 Joseph Bouchette surveyed Hull Township. Twelve thousand acres of land grants were given to Philemon Wright, Sr., and his three sons, Philemon, Tiberius, and Ruggles, as well as to James McConnell, Luthère Colton, Isaac Remic, Edmond Chamberlain, Harvey Parker, and Daniel Wyman. All these men and their descendants were to leave their imprint on the history and the landscape of the area. Aylmer, destined to become a bustling landing site for almost a century of river traffic, was founded largely on lumbering money and was the town of preference for government officials, land surveyors, and notaries, doctors, and other professionals.

If the rapids on the Ottawa — Chaudière, Little Chaudière, Remic, and Deschênes — were to prove the source of the early water power upon which the sawmill industries were based, they also presented serious obstacles to navigation and transportation. Three portages, carved out centuries earlier by the Algonquin Indians, were followed later by explorers, coureurs de bois, fur traders, missionaries, adventurers, first settlers, and early lumbermen.

When the fur brigades and timber raftsmen moored their craft at Aylmer, they were sometimes pretty unruly after so many months of loneliness away from civilization. When they reached Aylmer with its "easy drinking accesses and its fleshpots," the village would feel their fighting boastfulness. Once they had their skins full, they would begin to fight amongst themselves to see who was King of the River.

For the newcomers, although the river was the major highway, an overland route was also necessary. By 1805 a rough trail had been blazed between Hull and the landing site at Aylmer — a trail of history known today as the Aylmer Road and Main Street — down to the old landing site at Symmes Inn.

Those who first owned property near this boat landing were Ephraim Chamberlain, Harvey Parker, Daniel Wyman, and Ruggles and Tiberius Wright of Hull. Lot 21, Range 11, was leased in 1815 to Abel Reynolds, who in 1818 transferred his lease to Gideon and Zenus Olmstead, sons of Gideon Olmstead, who had settled on the Aylmer Road shortly after 1800 and was certainly one of the earliest settlers, if not *the* earliest, in the Aylmer area.

As the traffic increased on the river, Philemon Wright and sons of Hull built a store and a tavern at the landing. By 1820 the Turnpike Road had been completed up to a hotel at the landing, erected prior to 1822 by Wright for his nephew, Charles Symmes, an arrival from Symmes Corners near Boston, Massachusetts. Symmes wasted no time in his development of the village. He managed the inn and the store as well as his uncle's Chaudière Farm, surveyed and sold lots to immigrants, named streets, built his own residence, and finally in 1831 with a group of stock-holders built the first steamship on Lake Deschênes, the *Lady Colborne*. Four mornings a week she left Aylmer for Fitzroy Harbour; on off days she could be rented privately for towing lumber. Passenger service was extended above Chats Falls when the company launched its second steamship, the *George Buchanan*, to ply between the old trading posts of Fort William and Portage-du-Fort at the Chenaux (Snow) Falls.

By the 1830s the timber barons of Aylmer were beginning to put their stamp on Aylmer, both in grand residences and in business establishments. By 1840 Egan, Symmes, Conroy, and Harvey Parker, Sr., had begun a steam-powered flour and sawmill that greatly promoted Aylmer's commercial growth. After a period of fearsome lobbying with Hull, Aylmer was chosen as the seat of justice for Ottawa County.

The competition to the first sawmill arrived in quick succession as large sawmills operated by the Ritchies, the Baillies, the Cormiers, and the Frasers led to the expansion of Aylmer. In 1845 John Egan and Joseph Aumond formed the Union Forwarding Company and built the innovative iron steamer, the *Emerald*, deemed "fit for a king." Indeed, it was on this boat that the Prince of Wales (later Edward VII) made his trip upriver from Aylmer in 1860. The company's second ship, the *Oregon*, was launched above Chats Falls in 1864. But the extension of the Pontiac and Pacific Junction Railroad (the Push, Pull and Jerk) reached Aylmer in 1879 and sounded the demise of the colourful steamers. Aylmer lost its position as county town to Hull in the 1870s. By the 1890s the lumber trade on the Ottawa was dwindling and one by one the Aylmer sawmills began to close. The Hull Electric Railway, begun in Deschênes in 1896 by Robert and William Conroy, provided commuting services between Aylmer and

Ottawa, making it possible for Aylmer residents to both work and shop in the capital. As this trend increased, business in Aylmer suffered.

✳

It is only by resolving to maintain its "spirit of history" that Aylmer will preserve the distinctive character that sets it apart from all other areas of the Capital Region. Yet, in 1986, with a lack of vision that takes one's breath away, the Municipality of Aylmer turned its unique "Three Miles of History" — the Aylmer Road — into a four-lane highway into the town, affording the tourists little opportunity to "house-gaze" in the desperate hurry-up of Quebec traffic. However, if you stick to the right lane and try to dawdle, you can still glimpse the glory and grandeur of huge stone and brick mansions with their long, winding lanes leading back into the leisurely life of the nineteenth century, with its servants and horse-drawn carriages, its balls at Government House and visits to Quebec City for the timber-stand auctions.

The MacKay Wright House

A quarter-mile east of the T-turn onto the Aylmer Road from the Champlain Bridge rises a very imposing neo-classical stone mansion, backed by truly palatial stables on the hill, now all the headquarters of the Italian Embassy. Built about 1860 by MacKay Wright, a relative of Philemon Wright, the house was later occupied by E.B. Bessey, a grandson of E.B. Eddy, the Match King, and later by Elbert Soper, son of the great Ottawa electrical entrepreneur, Warren Soper.

Bellevue Cemetery

One mile west of the T-turn on the south side of the road, lies Bellevue Cemetery, like Inch Buie Cemetery at Arnprior, a history lesson in itself. Aylmer's early settlers, timber barons, surveyors, the marine men, and the all-important craftsmen and tradesmen who made up the early community keep company in this ancient burying ground. Gideon Olmstead gave the land for Bellevue with the stipulation that all denominations could be buried in it free of cost. That is, all but the Rollins family. Some old family feud, no doubt, is frozen in history here.

The Old McConnell Farm

Across from Bellevue Cemetery stands one of the many Aylmer district houses of the McConnell lumbering clan, the Old McConnell farmhouse. This warm, friendly, white frame Ontario house at 230 Aylmer Road was constructed toward the end of the nineteenth century for Conrad McConnell, grandson of James McConnell, who came to Hull in 1800. Several years ago the present owners, à la "Old McDonald Had a Farm," put up a prominent sign reading "The Old McConnell Farm" and on the front porch placed two old Québécois rocking chairs and, in them, two wonderful full-size effigies of Old McDonald and his wife. They turned out to be traffic-stoppers indeed, so much so that the owners had to remove the familiar and beloved characters from the veranda. "Too many accidents from people gaping as they went by," the owners told me when I asked them why.

¶ STORY

This story was told to me by the late George Roy of Ottawa:

When I worked on the Booth House on the Aylmer Road I met J.R. Booth every day. We had an awful time with him. You didn't know what was coming next. He'd change his mind and he got in wrong with the architects, and he didn't like them. He wouldn't consult them about anything and he wanted to do the planning himself. I shouldn't say this, but he raised his elbow a little too much too.

"I had five or six men with me from the Gillies house in Arnprior — we had just finished that — and we were running out of plans, and I didn't want to go ahead without them, and Booth was tearing around the country. So I got hold of him and said, 'Tomorrow morning you get into the architects and get the drawings out. If you don't, I'm taking my men back to Arnprior.' So he agreed, but the next morning he didn't show at all. I phoned the architects in Ottawa. 'Where the hell is he now?' I yelled. 'Oh, he's somewhere over in the States. He left last night!' "

*

The Old Rollins Home: *Rivermead*

About a mile and a half west of the bridge on the south side at 179 Aylmer Road sits Rivermead, a fine old stone, with lovely fanlights over the front door and an upstairs centre window. The house was built in 1842 for the Rollins family, but after 1870 was successively lived in by surveyors Edward Rainboth and John A. Snow, who was sent by the government of Canada to the Red River in 1869 to build a road toward Lake of the Woods and there became involved in difficulties with the Métis.

John Foran's Second House

On the north side of the highway just west of Rivermead, some distance from the road at the end of a tree-lined lane, stands a well-proportioned neo-classical stone house (*circa* 1858) with cut quoins and decorated eaves, built for lumberman John Foran, who came out from Ireland in 1820.

John Foran's First House

This lovely "Ontario vernacular" frame (*circa* 1826) at 156 Aylmer Road is without doubt one of the oldest houses in the Aylmer area.

The Samuel Stewart Homestead

Just east of Raceway Boulevard, the western entrance to the Connaught Jockey Club, sits the Samuel Stewart stone house, (*circa* 1850) still protected by its iron fencework.

The Charles Hurdman Homestead

One-half mile further down the Aylmer Road, just east of Deschênes Road (leading to Deschênes Rapids) is the Charles Hurdman homestead. A member of a prominent family in early settlement and in the timber trade, Hurdman is said to have introduced the use of the horse to the logging industry in place of the ox. Robert A.J. McConnell, one of the McConnell lumbering family, acquired the house in 1890.

The James McConnell II House

This vernacular Ontario stone house at 108 Aylmer Road was built in 1860 for Charles Hurdman, who had bought the property in 1818 from E. Chamberlain, one of the earliest settlers in the Aylmer area, arriving in Hull in 1800. In 1890 the property was sold to James McConnell, son of the scion of the McConnell lumbering family, James McConnell I.

The Richard McConnell House: *Woodlawn*

On the north side of the highway set back in extensive estate grounds is a cozy gabled homestead once known as Woodlawn, the home of Richard McConnell, early dealer in square timber. The house (*circa* 1850) was gutted during the great fires of August 1870, which burned on both sides of the Ottawa River and destroyed or damaged many of the old homes along the Aylmer Road and in the town itself. Woodlawn, reputed to have had the first inside toilet on the Aylmer Road, was furnished with fine Québécois furniture.

The James McConnell I House

One of the oldest stone houses along the Aylmer Road, this Ontario vernacular mansion at 84 Aylmer Road was built in 1820 for the original James McConnell, lumberman, who came from the United States in 1800 with Philemon Wright.

The Joseph McGoey House

On the south side at 41 Aylmer Road, a quarter-mile west of the turnoff to the village of Deschenes and the Deschenes Rapids, well back in the trees, there stands a large red brick Italianate home with considerable modern addition to the rear. It was constructed in 1871 for Joseph McGoey, a timber merchant from the Gatineau in the first half of the nineteenth century. In 1893 it was sold to Franklyn Grimes.

The Old Methodist Chapel

On the north side of the Aylmer Road, just beyond the McGoey House, is a simple Georgian stone building that was built originally as a Methodist chapel about 1826. Despite a number of renovations over the years, the shapes of the old roundheaded doors and window can still be detected in the masonry.

The Labelle House

On the north side of the Aylmer Road a short distance past the old Methodist chapel, just beyond Foley Street, is the Labelle House, a stone building that, until recently, lay in ruins after a fire. This somewhat Québécois-style building is said to have been used as early as 1828 as the first Roman Catholic meeting place in the Aylmer area. The Labelle House was made into a restaurant in 1977 and burned in 1979, but has now been restored with great care and true respect for the incomparable craftsmanship of the past.

Walking Tour of Aylmer

Along with Perth, Almonte, Lanark, Pembroke, and the towns of Glengarry County Williamstown, Summerstown, Lancaster — Aylmer is a town you will want to walk in. Park your car in one of the shopping centres (there are three) and begin your walk down the Aylmer Promenade.

Aylmer Promenade

The Aylmer Promenade begins at Market Square Park, at the junction of Main Street (Rue Principale) and the cutoff for the Eardley Road. The Old Court House (now the library), the New Court House, and the Dr. H.H.P. Hudson House (now a bar) are on the other three corners at the stoplights. Your walking tour of Aylmer proceeds down the Promenade with its tree-shaded boulevard, its elegant colonial-style lighting, and its softly muted, piped-in music.

A few years ago when the Quebec government, with some help

from the municipality of Aylmer, restored the exterior of historic Symmes Inn at the end of Main Street on the river, and renovated the interior, they also set up a system of grants for restoration in a designated circle around Symmes Inn. When this is done in other historic towns like Perth, Kingston, Quebec City, conditions are rigidly set out so that restorations are authentic. But, alas, Aylmer did not have such foresight and the result is that the heritage promenade houses, each with its own unique history, are restored, renovated, and rebuilt as a hodge-podge. Worse still, Aylmer zoned the houses on this stretch of Main Street as "commercial," so that all kinds of further desecrations are performed in the interest of running a business.

But there are positive aspects to this situation. Country Charm, for example, has done an exemplary restoration and, as a result, is attracting discriminating clientele from Ottawa as well as Aylmer and Hull.

Along the Promenade some of Aylmer's historic houses now contain a number of offices for notaries, land surveyors, the *Aylmer Bulletin*, as well as a judo school. In his old barbershop Chick goes back 60 years in catering to his Aylmer customers. Along this Promenade you can shop in a leisurely manner for health foods, cookies, children's clothing, high-fashion women's clothing, lingerie, kitchenware, wool, flowers, toys. You can drink at Danny's Bar or have espresso coffee and dessert at Café Près Bon Plein.

The Aylmer Academy (170 Main St.)

By mid-eighteenth century Aylmer was at an economic zenith and the building of these two old stones of Aylmer, the Aylmer Academy, next to the Methodist Church, is an early traditional marriage of church and school side by side, attesting to the wealth of the town at that time. Aylmer Academy was designed to be "a connecting link between the common school and college or university"; obviously the town fathers were looking toward higher education for their children, although they themselves may have been self-made men. The curriculum consisted of "the higher branches of arithmetic, algebra, geometry, English grammar, Latin and Greek Classics and elocution." The educational program was divided into three stages: the elementary level, the "model" or middle level, and the "academy" or most advanced

1 AYLMER ACADEMY 170 MAIN ST. 1861
2 HEATH HOUSE   178 MAIN ST. 1837
3 JOHN EGAN HOUSE 161 MAIN ST. 1840
4 COURT HOUSE 120 MAIN ST.   1852
5 MARKET SQUARE 1843
6 JUDGE McCORD HOUSE 10 BROAD ST. 1842
7 JOHN FORAN HOUSE   12 BROAD ST. 1850
8 THE HUDSON HOUSE 108 MAIN ST. 1914
9 JOHN WATT HOUSE 78 MAIN ST. 1870
10 THE BRITISH HOTEL 71 MAIN ST. 1841
11 CONROY-DRISCOLL HOUSE 72 MAIN ST. 1845
12 LAKEVIEW 61 MAIN ST. 1855
13 THE RENAULT-CHURCH HOUSE 66 MAIN ST. 1870
14 INGLIS HOUSE 62-64 MAIN ST. 1870
15 EDOUARD GRAVEL HOUSE

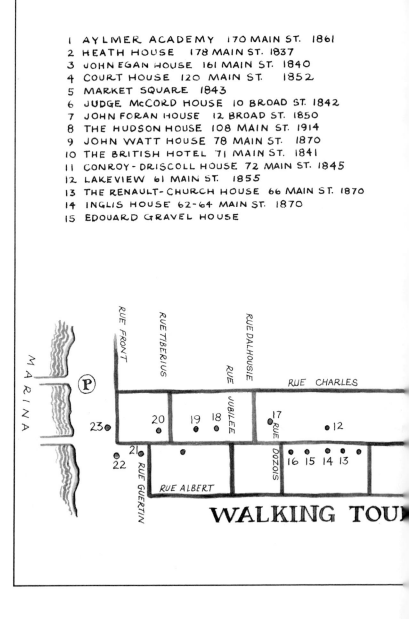

WALKING TOU

16　EPHRAIM GUIMOND HOUSE　58 MAIN ST.　1870
17　THE GEORGE McKAY HOUSE　53 MAIN ST.　1903
18　THE DR. EDMOND WOODS HOUSE:
　　CASTEL BLANC　43 MAIN ST.　1883
19　THE AMBROSE GOULET HOUSE　1885-86
20　THE BOLTON MEECH HOUSE　27 MAIN ST.　1860
21　THE KLOCK HOUSE　14 MAIN ST.　1870 or '80
22　THE JOHN McLEAN HOUSE　10 MAIN ST.　1840
23　SYMMES INN MAIN & FRONT STS.　1831

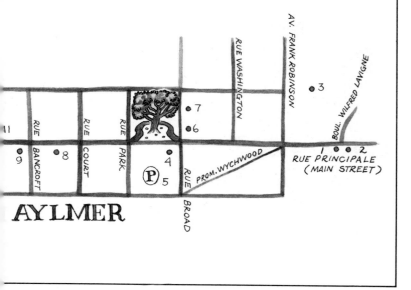

level. Both the church and the school have undergone a number of renovations after fires and restructuring for present-day needs.

Heath House (178 Main St.)

Set back from the street at the end of a long tree-lined driveway, this Georgian farmhouse dates from 1837. Simon Heath came to Hull Township in 1809. He married Matilda Chamberlain, a sister of Ephraim Chamberlain. The Heaths settled on Lot 20, Range 1, originally granted to Chamberlain in 1802.

During the decade 1840–50 the Methodist congregation of Aylmer approached leading citizens Charles Symmes and Ruggles Wright for the donation of land as a building site for parsonage and church. Both refused. Finally in 1851 Mrs. Simon Heath sold the Methodists a portion of her farm for the nominal sum of 10 pounds. The old Methodist chapel was sold as a private residence.

Heath House, built on the brink of a slope running to the river, has an unusual split-level construction with two storeys in the front and three behind. The house, with its many windows, was constructed of thin layers of shale stone quarried on the Heath farm.

The John Egan House: Mount Pleasant (161 Main St.)

It is fitting on this walking tour of Aylmer that you should early come to Mount Pleasant, John Egan's house, for this was indeed John Egan's town. Although he began his timber operations in the 1840s on the Upper Ottawa and was instrumental in the establishment of both Quyon and Eganville, Aylmer was really Egan's home base. Born in Ireland in 1811, Egan came to Aylmer in the 1830s and set up a general store. Elected as Aylmer's first mayor in 1847, MP at Quebec City from 1848 to 1857, Egan had extensive timber limits — at the time said to be second in extent only to those of J.R. Booth — making him a man of great influence and wealth throughout the Ottawa Valley. Mount Pleasant, built for Egan in 1840 on 30 acres of land purchased from John Wright, was probably unparalleled for its magnificence at that time. The large stone residence contained a second-storey ballroom where Egan entertained such illustrious guests as Lord Elgin in 1853 and Sir Edmund Head, the Governor-General, in 1856. At the age of 46 John Egan died tragically of cholera in Quebec City. It has been said that, had he not died so young, he would have surpassed J.R. Booth in his lumber operations.

Following Egan's death his home had a number of noteworthy owners. *The Canadian Illustrated News* sketch of the house in 1878 was done while under the ownership of Egan's son-in-law, W.R. Thistle. The property then passed in 1897 to timber baron William J. Conroy, who in turn sold it to Johnstone Edgerly. Edgerly was manager of the controversial Georgian Bay Ship Canal scheme, which proposed to construct a canal linking Georgian Bay with the Ottawa River at Mattawa. The scheme never came to fruition, but every few years or so the dream is revived.

Robert H. Wright, a grandson of John Wright, the original land-owner, bought the house in 1909. Mayor of Aylmer (1907–11), Wright supplied his florist shop in Ottawa with seedlings grown in a vast four-acre complex of greenhouses located near the house. The coal to heat the greenhouses was trucked in via CPR by means of a private railway spur that came up Mountain Street and entered the property through the west gate. In 1933 the estate was sold to the Redemptorist Order, which erected the enormous stone seminary at the rear of the house.

The Courthouse (120 Main St.)

If Ruggles Wright wouldn't give land for the Methodist Church and parsonage, he did come through for the courthouse, deeding the land to the government in 1850. The second courthouse, serving the counties of Ottawa and Pontiac, was constructed in 1852. It contained the County Registry Office and also the prison, dubbed "The Dark Hole" by those who knew it all too well. The 1878 sketch from *The Canadian Illustrated News* shows the 12-foot-high stone wall that surrounded the prison yard at that time.

When County Court was moved to Hull in 1897, the government donated the courthouse to the town of Aylmer, which has used it ever since as a town hall.

Market Square

The centre of history in Aylmer, the Market Square property was sold to the town by Charles Symmes in 1853 and, although it was intended as a marketplace where farmers and truck gardeners from along the Eardley Road could sell their produce, the square became the social meeting place for villagers as well as the legal centre of the town, surrounded as it was by the courthouse, the town hall, and the prison. Notaries and lawyers found the square to be an ideal spot around which to establish their residences and offices.

The Judge McCord House (10 Broad St.)

As Diane Aldred explains in her book *Aylmer: Its Heritage*, William King McCord came to live in Aylmer when he was appointed judge of the Circuit Court in 1842. He immediately had built for him on the park right across from the courthouse this fine old colonial American saltbox, framed with square timbers. Historian J.L. Gourlay recalls that Judge McCord was very talented and full of humour. Gourlay tells the story of one wintry day when they encountered each other in front of the Aylmer Post Office. McCord jokingly made some comparisons between their noses, pointing out that his was so full of brandy that the snowflakes "fizzled off it like raindrops off a hot iron." By contrast, he said, those of Reverend Gourlay's nose "stuck till thawed off by natural heat."

Until his death in 1858 McCord was a renowned character of Aylmer. His son Thomas, also an advocate and later a judge, inherited the property; his law office was entered by the smaller of the two front doors.

In 1870 the house passed to Alexander Bourgeau, who became another local director of the Upper Ottawa Steamship Company and mayor of Aylmer in 1872 and 1880.

Now a private residence, the house has been lovingly restored and preserved by two generations of a family that has a real respect for the "spirit of history" in Aylmer and the workmanship of the craftsmen of the past.

The John Foran House (12 Broad St.)

Jean Delisle was another early Aylmer advocate who found living on the park across from his work very convenient. A door on the south side of the neo-classical frame house led to his office, which was located in the southwest corner. The two-and-half-storey house constructed of hand-hewn square timbers was built for

AYLMER TOWN HALL (THE OLD COURTHOUSE)

Constructed in 1852, this building served as the courthouse for Ottawa and Pontiac Counties until 1897, when county court was moved to Hull. (Photo courtesy the Town of Aylmer.)

Delisle in the early 1850s.

In the mid-1860s the house passed to John Murphy, steamboat captain for the Union Forwarding Company. The house was then inherited by Murphy's widow, Abigail Dramper, who sold it in 1883 to lumberman John Foran. Like a number of other successful lumbermen, Foran left his large stone house on the Aylmer Road and moved to town to spend his later years. The house is now a private residence of a legal family, and, like the McCord House, is being restored by people with a truly educated appreciation for an invaluable heritage.

Together the McCord House and the Delisle House make up the Priceless Pair of Aylmer Square.

The Hudson House (108 Main St.)

Dr. H.P. Hudson came from Chelsea just after the turn of the century to practice medicine in Aylmer. This huge brick house on the park was built for him in 1914. It is now Danny's Bar, so you can go in and imagine how grand it once was.

The John Watt House (78 Main St.)

Badly battered, this large frame house with its fairly recent pillars stands on the site of the first hotel in Aylmer and predates Symmes Inn (*circa* 1832). The original building was constructed for the Wrights in 1822 and in that year prepared for the arrival of Charles Symmes from Hull. The old hotel was then run as a stopping-place successively by George Bolton, Robert Conroy, and finally Charles McCarthy. John Watt, a blacksmith from across the Ottawa in March Township, settled on the property in the early 1880s and married Anna McCloy of Aylmer whose father, Thomas, deeded the land to the couple in the early 1900s.

The back of the house with its lovely pillared downstairs and upstairs verandas escaped the fire of the 1890s and is believed to have been an addition made to the original 1822 stopping-place. This house now contains the offices of land surveyors.

The Conroy–Driscoll House (72 Main St.)

In 1837 merchant and lumberman Robert Conroy married Mary McConnell, daughter of the McConnell lumbering family, thus fulfilling one of the established traditions of the Ottawa Valley "gentry": lumber money marrying lumber money. The newly-weds lived first in an apartment in the hotel at 76 Main and then moved in 1841 to an apartment in their newly completed British Hotel at 71 Main. Conroy is understood to have had the two-storey stone at 72 Main completed in 1845 as a first residence for his growing family. After 1881 the house was then lived in succes-sively by Alfred Driscoll, a provincial land surveyor and son-in-law of Conroy; by Robert Driscoll, Alfred's son who married Mary Martin, a daughter of William Martin; and by Dr. Robert Martin. Dr. Martin was later joined by his brother Archie Martin, who had returned to Aylmer after having spent most of his life in the Yukon prospecting for gold. It now houses a bake shop, a chic dress boutique, and a very exclusive children's clothing shop.

The British Hotel (71 Main St.)

Like Symmes, Egan, and Foran, Robert Conroy left his mark on Aylmer with more than one heritage building. The British Hotel, one of the great historic hotels left in the Ottawa Valley, was built in 1841 for him seven years after he had opened his first hotel across the street. An outstanding entrepreneur, Conroy ran two more businesses from the back yard of the British Hotel: during the 1840s Moses Holt drove Conroy's stagecoaches from the hotel to connect with the steamboat landing in Hull, and the hotel's livery stables contained horses and carriages that could be rented by travellers "at the shortest notice."

A large extension on the east side, incorporating the arched carriageway, was added to the older half of the hotel in the 1840s. The expanded building contained "four elegantly furnished pub-lic parlours," a "spacious and elegant hall fitted up in the best manner for parties and balls," and "a bar with the best brands of liquors, wines and cigars." By the 1850s Conroy was absorbed in his thriving lumber business, and the hotel began to pass through a succession of hands, including those of the celebrated I.C. Macrow, who had created Macrow's Celebrated Wormwood Bit-ters, famous on the travelling medicine man circuits.

This version was told to me by Pierre-Louis Lapointe, an archivist at the Quebec Government Archives in Hull:

Thomas D'Arcy McGee was assassinated in Bytown on April 6, 1868. That same night there was a Conroy wake being held in the parlour of the British American Hotel in Aylmer. Suddenly four men burst into the wake room, leaving their exhausted horses at the door foaming at the mouth. They were all strangers, very anxious, watching the door all the time, checking their watches frequently, and nobody could understand why they had come to Conroy's wake. But it was said later that they were really the assassins of Thomas D'Arcy McGee, come to establish their alibi in Aylmer."

✻

Lakeview (61 Main St.)

As the ultimate public manifestation of his prosperity and success, Robert Conroy had this stone building constructed as his second house in 1855. It did indeed once command an unbroken view of Lake Deschênes and the colourful river traffic of those early days when "the River was the Highway."

By this time Conroy was a renowned lumber merchant whose sawmill in Deschênes during the 1850s formed the nucleus around which the village grew. He also served as Aylmer's fourth mayor until his death in 1868.

Surrounded by two acres of lawn and gardens, the large Georgian style-stone mansion was distinguished not only by superior construction but also by immense rooms, three handsome fireplaces, and finely carved wood panelling lining all the deep interior window recesses. From the library a door opened into a large conservatory.

The Conroy family kept Lakeview until 1915. Now, sadly declined, it has been turned into a discotheque.

The Inglis House (62–64 Main St.)

This little stucco-covered tradesman's double was constructed of 12-inch timbers in 1870. William and Hiram Inglis ran a general store and bakery in the west half of the building, with living quarters in the east half and above the store. In 1940 the property was purchased by Gerald Lajoie, an employee of timber king J.R. Booth.

The Denault–Church House (66 Main St.)

This log house was evidently built for tradesman Ferrier Denault, a carpenter who moved here from Charles Street around 1870. He rented the house for a number of years to Theodore A. Howard, one of Aylmer's first druggists who came to Aylmer from Montreal in 1870.

The Edouard Gravel House (60 Main St.)

This third log tradesman's house was erected in the 1870s by Edouard Gravel, one of four brothers, all tinsmiths, who came to Aylmer in the early 1850s. The aluminum siding was put on in 1976.

The Ephraim Guimond House (58 Main St.)

Another one of the many historic Aylmer log houses now covered with aluminum siding, this tradesman's house was built around 1870 for Ephraim Guimond, sometime innkeeper at Symmes Inn during the decade. After 1878, having learned it all at Symmes Inn, Mr. Guimond began his own tavern business here.

The George McKay House (53 Main St.)

At the turn of the century, on his way up and ultimately headed for bigger things in Ottawa, George McKay came to Aylmer from Quyon, where he had run the sawmill started by his father in 1867. In 1903 he had this impressive brick with its circular corner porch and widow's walk built on the corner of Main and Dalhousie. Originally the extensive property, stretching back to Charles Street, included gardens and orchards, stables, sheds, and a coachhouse. McKay lived in Aylmer only a few years before going to Ottawa. His house was sold to Thomas Ritchie, Sr., who operated another Aylmer sawmill business. The house is now an office for notaries.

Dr. Edmond Woods' House: *Castel Blanc* (43 Main St.)

Although this Pittoresque example of architecture has lost much of its Victorian detail since its construction in 1883, it remains residential and is one of the most charming of the Aylmer frame heritage houses. John Robert Woods, a native of Sainte-Marie-du-Manoir, Quebec, came to Aylmer around 1840. Woods ran a general store with the post office on Main Street for over 50 years until his death in 1895. In 1847 he married Zoe Desautels, a sister of Father Desautels, St. Paul's first parish priest. Their eldest son, Dr. J.J.E. Woods, a graduate of McGill University in 1875, had this house built shortly after his marriage to Corinne Bourgeois, daughter of Judge B. Bourgeois. Mayor of Aylmer for one term, Dr. Woods practiced medicine from his home office until he moved to Lachine, Quebec, as Inspector of Asylums and Jails in 1918. After his death in Lachine in 1928 Mrs. Woods returned to this house and lived with her daughter and son-in-law, Mr. and Mrs. Rodolphe Maltais. The house remained in the Maltais family until 1973.

The Ambrose Goulet House (41 Main St.)

Ambrose Goulet was another one of those many people attracted to Aylmer in the early days because of the steamboat business. He came in 1868 to work as an engineer for the Union Forwarding Company. In 1881 when that company sold its holdings to the Upper Ottawa Improvement Company (the ICO), Goulet bought a small fleet of steamboats that plied the Ottawa until the 1890s. In 1888 he built the steamship *Albert*, which towed log booms on the river until 1917, when it was dismantled at the Quyon docks, sounding the death knell of the river as highway. When steam died at Aylmer, Goulet moved to Beaubarnois, Quebec, to work.

At the height of his prosperity, Goulet had this large brick constructed for him in 1885–86. Originally the house had gracious mansard roof, front veranda, and rounded third-storey windows with fine decorative trim. Not much is recognizable today as it lives an apartment life.

The Bolton–Meech House (27 Main St.)

This two-storey house erected in 1860 is the oldest brick in Aylmer. Like its neighbouring Kenny house, it, too, was virtually built to "last forever." The exterior walls of double-brick thickness were built of rows of brick ends alternating with rows of brick lengths, forming not only an attractive design but also an exceptionally solid construction.

Acquired by the Horatio Cahill family around 1870, the house served for more than 30 years as the residence of George Cahill Bolton, captain of the renowned steamship *Jason Gould* during the 1860s.

In 1917 the house again became the property of a family that contributed greatly to the early history of the Ottawa Valley when it was purchased by Alfred Meech, for many years manager of the Hull Electric Railway. Mr. Meech was the grandson of the famous early preacher Asa Meech of Chelsea. The daughter-in-law of Asa Meech, Mrs. Meech lived here until her death in 1971.

The Klock House (14 Main St.)

Although generally known as the Klock House, this great Princess Anne Victorian brick may have been built in the 1870s for Alexis Rajotee, who came to Aylmer from Sorel, Quebec, in 1856 and opened a general store on Main Street. By 1870 he had become captain of the steamship *Monitor* and treasurer for the Upper Ottawa Steamboat Company. James Klock, a prosperous trader and farmer, lived here from 1881 until he sold it in the late 1890s to S.F.E. Ritchie, owner of the Ritchie sawmill at Deschênes.

It is another outstanding example of Victorian solidity, featuring plank-on-plank construction. All interior and exterior walls are built of one-inch-thick boards laid flat and stacked one upon the other as high as the roofline. These planks, seven inches wide each, formed a thick wall over which the brick siding was applied. Each alternate plank was indented, forming an uneven surface to which the plaster could easily adhere. Two major factors were probably responsible for this type of construction in the Aylmer area: the availability of cheap lumber and the influence of so many people who "worked in wood."

The John McLean House (10 Main St.)

One of the unique houses of the Ottawa Valley — indeed in the whole of Canada — this house is said to have been erected by the Union Forwarding Company as a residence for its business agent in the 1840s. The most outstanding feature of the old house is its unusual wood siding, which is scored to resemble the much more expensive cut-stone construction. Even such details as lintel stones over the windows and cut cornerstones or quoins have been carefully simulated by clever craftsmen to look like cut stone. Only two other buildings in Quebec and Ontario are known to have exteriors similar to this.

In the late 1850s the company sold the house to John McLean, who had come to Aylmer in 1846 to work as an engineer aboard the company's first steamship, the *Emerald*. By the time he purchased the house, John McLean was married to Mary Elizabeth Hall, niece of Mrs. Charles Carey Symmes. Three generations of their descendants lived in this house until recently. In June 1988 this heritage house was designated the new Aylmer Museum.

Symmes Inn (Main and Front Sts.)

Symmes Inn, one of the crowning glories of the Quebec government's heritage endeavours in the past decade, stands today on the Ottawa River at the foot of Main Street, salvaged from ruins and restored to the tune of $1,700,000.

The Promenade ends at Symmes Inn. A superlative French cuisine dining room serves Sunday brunch so popular that you must make reservations a week ahead; dinner only is served all week long. You can stop in and have a quiet drink in the cool, slate-floored downstairs, or on a lovely summer day climb to the upstairs veranda overlooking the Ottawa River, the beginning of the walking and cycling path, and the Aylmer Yacht Club and Marina. The *Nelson*, a tourist boat, leaves the Marina daily and heads upriver. The boat holds 90 people, takes hourly tours, and accommodates party bookings.

HISTORY

One of Aylmer's men of vision and earliest entrepreneurs, Charles Symmes had this huge stone hotel built on the waterfront in 1831 in anticipation of the steamship service that was established in 1832. It is safe to assume that Symmes Inn must have been a most welcome sight to every sort of river traveller coureurs de bois, fur traders, Hudson Bay men in their canoes, and freight

SYMMES INN

Aylmer founding father Charles Symmes built this hotel in 1831 to serve the steamship trade on the Ottawa River. The building has been carefully restored and integrated into the Aylmer waterfront development. (Photo courtesy the Town of Aylmer.)

canoes; passengers off the steamers plying the Ottawa River between Bytown and Fitzroy Harbour; travellers off the stagecoach that ran regularly between Symmes Inn and Bedard's Inn in Hull, enabling people from Montreal to connect with the *Lady Colborne* and the Upper Ottawa. No doubt the rooms, the great verandas overlooking Lake Deschênes, and the hotel yard are haunted by the history makers: timber barons Gillies and Gilmore, Booth and Edwards, going up or coming down from their camps to the north; with the great rivermen "off the Drive," Mountain Jack Thomson, Gentleman Paddy Dillon, Larry Frost, Joseph Montferrand; with infamous characters like Peter Aylen, "King of the Shiners," and his giant bodyguard, Martin Hennessy of Pembroke.

A SIDE TOUR OF HERITAGE BUILDINGS

You are now at the end of Aylmer's Promenade but Old Aylmer is full of more heritage buildings. Perhaps you might like to walk up Court Street to see one of the last remaining streets of "Worker's Houses" still left in the whole area, some of them now being updated. Or seek out the old log houses of Aylmer, albeit most of them covered, camouflaged, and disguised. Aylmer is one of the few towns in the whole Ottawa Valley with a heritage of log houses that, if uncovered and cared for, could make the town a unique tourist attraction. The only other town in the Valley with comparable streetscapes lined with original log buildings was Nickabeau, above Chapeau, Quebec. But the hurricane of August 1985 wiped out most of the hamlet's log heritage.

Christ Church and Rectory (101-103 Charles St.)

The Anglican Christ Church, the only one of Aylmer's old churches to have escaped damage or destruction by fire, was built in 1840 on land donated by Charles Symmes. The white frame rectory next door was erected in 1868. Among the many memorials in the church are the richly coloured stained-glass windows and marble wall plaques raised well over a century ago to honour two major supporters, lumbermen John Egan and Robert Conroy.

The Joseph Leclerc and Welsh–O'Donnell Houses
(41–43 Notre Dame)

Of these two neighbouring camouflaged original log houses, No. 41 has the more interesting story, for here, once upon a time, lived a renowned shantyman, Joseph Leclerc, who is said to have inherited from the legendary Joseph Montferrand the reputation of being the "strongest man in the Ottawa Valley." Leclerc came to Aylmer in 1850 and had this log house built for his family about 1860. The house remained in the family for almost a century, occupied after Leclerc's death first by his son, Jean, who returned to Aylmer after having spent many years in the Yukon in the search for gold. No. 43 Notre Dame was erected for James Welsh shortly after his arrival in Aylmer from Ireland in 1852.

The Peter Aylen, Sr., House (108 Albert St.)

This house is important primarily because in the 1850s it was the residence of lumberman Peter Aylen, known as "King of the Shiners." At this time in his life he had relinquished leadership of the Irish shantymen in Bytown and retired to Aylmer to become a pillar of society.

HISTORY

Bytown in the spring was always torn apart by an invasion of raftsmen and shantymen from "up the Valley," roisterering, rioting, brawling, and drinking in the streets of the town, and often savagely beating, even sometimes killing, anyone who dared to challenge them. For weeks at the end of "the Drive" the town customarily suffered this "reign of terror" when all respectable inhabitants kept indoors.

This disorganized violence in 1835 found a leader in Peter Aylen, an Irishman who came to Canada from Ireland as a sailor, jumped ship at Quebec, changed his name, and disappeared into the forests of the Upper Ottawa River. Aylen began his lumber business in 1816, and by the time of the peak of the Shiners' War, 1835–37, Aylen owned property in Bytown, Nepean, and Horton townships and had large timber operations on the Madawaska, Bonnechere, and Gatineau rivers.

In 1835, for reasons that even today appear obscure, the well-to-do Aylen assumed leadership of the Irish shantymen, organizing their traditional violence to drive the French Canadians off the river and thus guarantee more jobs and higher wages for the Irish in the timber camps. He offered seductive lures to his followers: jobs in his shanties and in those of his friends; promises of a complete victory over the French Canadians; and, for a people all too familiar with poverty, lavish feasting and drinking always available at the Shiner leader's home in Bytown. Indeed, women were often supplied to the shantymen and raftsmen after their long winter months of enforced celibacy; it was even reported that on some occasions Aylen imported prostitutes from Montreal for his followers. The orgies at the King's home were legendary debaucheries.

For two years Peter Aylen led his Shiners in organized violence, assault and battery, beatings and murders, ambushes and attacks in the night that intimidated all municipal authority and broke down all forces of civilization. It was not until the Rebellion winter of 1837–38 that the forces of law and order gathered themselves together enough to quell the insurgent Shiners. Sensing a new mood, Aylen sold his property in Bytown and moved to Aylmer, where he became a leading citizen of the town and a veritable tower of respectability.

After Aylen's death in 1868, the house was inherited by his second son, John, who was both a doctor and a lawyer in Aylmer.

DIRECTIONS

You can retrace your steps back along the Aylmer Road and return to Ottawa across the Champlain Bridge. Or you can start a tour of the Pontiac, described in the next chapter.

Chapter 5

UP THE PONTIAC!

Preamble

L ike the Colossus at Rhodes, the Ottawa Valley straddles two sides of the Ottawa River, with one foot in Eastern Ontario and the other in Western Quebec.

In the beginning, Western Quebec was a thin riverside strip of tiny villages and fledgling farming settlements, backed by a huge, amorphous, timbered wilderness destined to be a "jewel box" for the timber barons, the Laurentian Mountains, and an estimated 4,000 lakes providing vast and often inaccessible hunting and fishing preserves.

Today the trees are mere "sticks" and the fish fewer, but nothing much has really changed in Pontiac County. Only 20,000 people live in the band of land running along the river from just outside Aylmer to Des Joachims (The Swisha), and the rest of one of the largest counties in Quebec, 24,000 square kilometres, is still an enormous wilderness "park."

1 CHAMPLAIN BRIDGE
2 AYLMER
3 EARDLEY ROAD (ROUTE 148)
4 LUSKVILLE
5 STE. CECILE DE MASHAM
6 QUYON
7 NORWAY BAY
8 BRISTOL
9 SHAWVILLE
10 CHARTERIS
11 LADYSMITH
12 THORNE CENTRE
13 SCHWARTZ
14 PORTAGE DU FORT
15 BRYSON
16 CAMPBELL'S BAY
17 DANFORD LAKE
18 KAZABAZUA

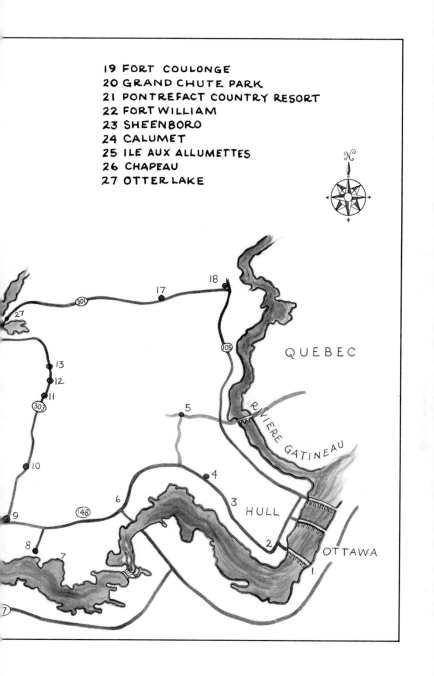

19 FORT COULONGE
20 GRAND CHUTE PARK
21 PONTREFACT COUNTRY RESORT
22 FORT WILLIAM
23 SHEENBORO
24 CALUMET
25 ILE AUX ALLUMETTES
26 CHAPEAU
27 OTTER LAKE

QUEBEC

RIVIÈRE GATINEAU

HULL

OTTAWA

When you set out to explore the treasures of Western Quebec, be forewarned. There are fewer villages and the roads are fewer and farther between, more twisting and winding, frequently haphazardly marked — or not at all. Therefore, you should carry a good map of Western Quebec. Since much of it is bush, there's often no way of cutting across country on concession roads, as you can on the Ontario side of the river.

Although Western Quebec was settled largely by Anglo-Saxons, the population ratio is changing, and you should also take along your bilingualism or a French-English dictionary for places like Aylmer, Quyon, and Fort Coulonge.

There are very few good eating places in Western Quebec, so you should pack picnics for some of the truly lovely wayside *haltes* (parks) and beaches along the way. Or wait until you get to Meilleur's Hotel in Chapeau.

DIRECTIONS

If you start from Ottawa, take the Queensway to Island Park Drive, cross over the Champlain Bridge to the Quebec side, and at the first stoplights turn left and head toward Aylmer.

If you start your trip up the Pontiac from Aylmer, take the Eardley Road, Highway No. 148, through the town and keep going.

You will be following that highway almost entirely, except for any side excursions you choose. On Aylmer's outskirts you enter Pontiac County.

Eardley Road Country Houses

A narrow, tortuous, ill-cared-for road with a ridiculous speed limit (seldom observed), the route between Aylmer and Quyon affords the traveller some wonderful wide sweeps of the Ottawa River in a more tranquil mood as it makes its leisurely way from the tumult at Chaudière Falls to the tumult awaiting it at Chats Falls (Arnprior) and Fitzroy Harbour. I have driven this road thousands of times but always view with renewed wonder this panoramic span of the river, never failing to imagine the astonishment which those first explorers — Nicholas Vignau, Champlain, Coulonge — in their frail canoes must have looked upon this untouched world.

As the road moves away from the river and draws excitingly close to the shadows of the mountains, some of the richest farming land in the Valley — the Eardley Flats — runs verdantly riverward. Along the Eardley Road, particularly just outside Aylmer, rich alluvial clay was deposited by the retreat of the ice sheets thousands of years ago. A few truck gardens are still tended, but in the earlier days a greater part of the fresh produce of Ottawa's famous Byward Market was transported from these market gardens and nurseries.

The riverside is now lined with cottages, some of them very old, with new houses crowding in to get a piece of the valuable riverfront or a view of the mighty "Grand," as the Ottawa was originally called.

HISTORY

From 1786 to 1800 Joseph Mondion, the first white settler of the Pontiac, lived on a point of land half a mile below the Chats Rapids at Fitzroy Harbour. He kept a trading post and, in order to attract more business, cultivated what is believed to be the first white man's farm in the country, the fresh garden produce of which he sold to the Indians and *voyageurs* alike. Later the North West Company took over, and in 1821 John McLean became the Hudson Bay Company factor.

The next permanent settlements occurred in 1818: the Balmer Brothers, who were to become well-known lumbermen, settled on Ghost Hill; Joseph Lusk took up the land near present-day Luskville, named for him; and Andrew Telfer from Scotland moved into the Clarendon area around Shawville. Cuthbertsons, with the Gaelic, and the Dodds were amongst the first into the Norway Bay–Bristol area.

On the immediate outskirts of Aylmer along the Eardley Road (Highway No. 148) sit some of the original manor houses of the first settlers: Foran, McLean, Church, Parker, and Lusk, some of whom were given huge grants of land that ran from the moun-

111

tains to the river. If you can take your eyes off the glorious view to your right, you will see the houses that tell the history.

The Church House (100 Eardley Road)

Dr. Peter Howard Church came from Leeds County, Upper Canada, to the Aylmer area, and in 1832 had this one-and-a-half-storey log house built for his family on the river side of the Eardley Road. When he failed to make a living there and threatened to move on, the families of the area responded by subscribing an annual sum, whether sick or not, in order to keep their doctor in the district. In 1846 Dr. Church received his second degree in medicine from McGill University.

Dr. Church's three sons, Coller, Howard, and Ruggles, also graduated in medicine from McGill, as did seven of their descendants. Indeed, for over a century, until 1955, there was a Dr. Church practicing in Aylmer — just as for well over a century there was a Father Harrington at Chapeau. Ruggles Church, with degrees in both law and medicine, practiced law early in his career in Aylmer with the firm of Fleming, Church, and Kenney.

The house remained in the Church family until 1880, when the then Dr. Church moved into Aylmer and the house was purchased by Thomas P. Foran, a son of lumberman John Foran and the first lawyer to graduate from the University of Ottawa in 1865.

The Harvey Parker, Jr., House (130 Eardley Road)

Harvey Parker, Sr., arrived from the United States in 1801. He married Azenath Chamberlain, a sister of first settler Ephraim Chamberlain. Together they carved out a 170-acre riverfront farm and raised a family. This large frame house was built on the farm by Parker for his eldest son during the 1840s. The house remained in the family until 1910 when it was sold to "Klondike" George Mulligan. During the 1930s the Harvey Hoppers ran a successful tea room there. The house has been largely altered and added to by successive owners.

The William McLean House

In 1851 at the age of 26, William McLean came to Aylmer with his brother John and established a general store and tannery that was a landmark on Main Street for many years. A much-respected member of the community and Aylmer's fifth mayor for two consecutive terms, William McLean was chosen to deliver the welcome address to the Prince of Wales on his stopover at Aylmer during his 1860 tour of the Ottawa.

In the 1860s the McLean brothers began operating the Aylmer Steam Sawmill, which provided the lumber for this, another of the plank-on-plank houses in the Aylmer area. The house is identical in design to the rectory of Christ Church, built also about the same time and of the same materials.

The James F. Taylor House

Born in Scotland, James Finlayson Taylor came to Hull in the early 1800s to work at his trade as a blacksmith but also as bookkeeper for Philemon Wright. A staunch Methodist, Taylor was instrumental in the building of the old stone Methodist Chapel on the Aylmer Road, *circa* 1826.

Taylor married three times, never failing to make "good connections." His first wife, Mary Wright, a daughter of his boss, Philemon Wright, died in 1831. His second marriage to Nancy Olmstead, daughter of first settler Gideon Olmstead, ended in her death in 1837. Elizabeth Edey, a daughter of Moses Edey, in 1842 became his third wife.

This log house, now covered with clapboard, was built on a portion of Moses Edey's homestead, which he had settled in 1806. When Taylor died in 1868 at the age of 87, he had become one of the most influential and respected members of the Aylmer community. He is buried in nearby Edey Cemetery.

Between the first Church house on the Eardley Road in Aylmer and Breckenridge there are three outstanding stone houses overlooking the Ottawa.

The Michael Foran House

On the south side of the road, nearly four miles out of Aylmer, stands the first Foran old stone, two and half storeys high, very unadorned but with modern shutters added, dating from 1860.

The Foran House

On the river side of the Eardley Road, four and a half miles from the Church house, stands another old stone, this time only a storey and a half high, also belonging to the Foran clan. The stone is very well cut and the veranda has a curved roof.

The Hurdman House

Five and a half miles from the Church house, on the mountain side of the road, stands a slightly larger house with verandas two storeys high at the front. It was built for James Hurdman about 1861. The legend is that some sort of rivalry existed between Hurdman and his neighbour Foran, and Hurdman is said to have deliberately built his house larger than Foran's to prove some point now buried with both of them.

Ghost Hill

S omewhere along this stretch of Eardley Road, high up on the height of land, it is said that certain perspicacious people can still find traces of the Old Indian Trail with its lookouts spaced along it, used by the Algonquin Indians (the first settlers in this area on Calumet Island about 1600) to observe the approach of their enemies, the Iroquois, or the movements of those white strangers. So watch for the ghosts of the Indians!

Pontiac County was settled by the Scots, English, French, Germans, Poles, and Irish — but mostly, from the Eardley Road to Sheenboro, by the Irish, the superstitious, folkloric Irish. Perhaps this accounts for the richness of the ghost stories that haunt the countryside: the Ghost of Greermount, the Ghost Girl of the Picanoc (both back of Shawville), the Ghost Daggs of Shawville, and, the most famous of all, the thronging ghosts of Ghost Hill near Breckenridge.

Along Highway No. 148, just south of Breckenridge bridge, St. Augustine's Anglican Church (*circa* 1874), now a residence, virtually sits on the highway. Just past this site is Ghost Hill, a long,

GHOST HILL FARM

Situated on Hignway No. 148 just past Breckenridge is Ghost Hill Farm. This old stone is the focus of any number of haunting tales about ghosts and witches.

sweeping grade with mysteriously tangled bush on both sides, and, at the top of the hill, as you go down toward the bridge, an easy-to-miss laneway leading up to the Lusk House on Ghost Hill, an old stone almost hidden from view at the foot of the Gatineaus.

Since early childhood, travelling up Highway No. 148 long before it was paved from Ottawa to Shawville, I had always viewed that road between the mountains and the river with a sense of awe — not only with reverence before its beauty but also with a suspicion of its haunted and supernatural aspects. I was not the least surprised when I heard about the Witches of Eardley from my older people, and even less so when I read about them in Anson Gard's book about the countryside written 80 years ago.

❦ STORIES

These are some of the stories told by the oldtimers along the Eardley Road:

Since the 1800s, along this stretch of Highway No. 148, weird things have happened both in broad daylight and in the dead of the night. White-faced farmers raced home to tell of wagon wheels that refused to go up Ghost Hill. Horses there took sudden fright and upset carts and drivers, sometimes injuring them. Eerie and inexplicable noises were heard in the trees on both sides of Ghost Hill and, not infrequently, a strange light would be seen by teamsters a few yards in front of their horses, only to disappear as the driver approached it. Even more frightening, travellers on the road said that sometimes the eerie lights would move from in front of the horses to behind the rig or wagon. One man saw the Devil jump into his cart, horns, tail, spear, and all. Many people have reported over almost two centuries of hearing wailing sounds or seeing white filmy figures floating along the edges of the road at Ghost Hill.

✻

Early in the 1800s on a gloomy, grey autumn day a young man went walking in the woods in the Luskville area with his gun. At Ghost Hill in the distance he saw a cow approaching, but when it started to charge at him in a peculiar way he realized there was something wrong with it and he shot it. When he got up to the cow, much to his horror he discovered he

116

had shot his best friend, who had put on a cow's hide to play a practical joke. The body of the practical joker disappeared and his soul was said to have gone into an old gnarled tree that stood on the site of the tragedy. The tree became haunted with the soul of the dead young man. So many district accidents were attributed to the ghost in the old gnarled tree that finally, in 1830, Pioneer Lusk had to cut it down to get rid of the hex.

✳

An Eardley farmer for a long while had failed to get any butter from his churnings. He would have the whole family take turns at the old dasher but, try as they might, none of them could make the butter "come."

"Why don't you send for the witch doctor? Your cows are obviously bewitched," said a neighbour.

The farmer, who was an educated man, laughed at such a foolish suggestion. But finally in desperation, "for the fun of it," as he put it, he sent for the Witch of Eardley, and after the visitation the farmer's butter would "come regular."

Now, no harm would have come of this whole thing, except that the witch, in order to prove her ability, told the farmer that the man who had bewitched his cows would come to visit him within eight days to borrow something.

Well, within eight days of the witch's forecast, one of the farmer's most trusted neighbours ran out of beans and came over to borrow some. And right then and there the farmer broke off the friendship of a lifetime with his neighbour.

And it is said that the borrowing of beans in Eardley has been quite unknown from that time to this.

Farther Up the Pontiac

Luskville

Luskville provides good "swimming holes" on the Ottawa River as well as picnic areas and pastoral scenery. The beach here was once a favourite stopover for the Indians travelling upriver.

Archaeological diggings in 1934 uncovered a number of artifacts. If you're lucky, you still might find an arrowhead or pieces of pottery.

Luskville Falls

Located on the mountain side of the road is a National Capital Commission mini-park on the fringes of the Gatineau Park. Look for the sign on Highway No. 148 that says "Ste-Cecile-de-Masham." The park has picnic tables with barbecues, split wood, water, outdoor toilets, as well as a quiet grassy site beside a waterfall that is especially lovely in the spring. There is blueberry picking in July and August, relaxation under old pine trees, and, for the very energetic, trail climbing. The trail, which winds up to a fire ranger's lookout, is sometimes steep but never treacherous; you can complete the climb in about 30 minutes and enjoy the splendid view downriver to the nation's capital and upriver about 50 miles to Pembroke.

Quyon

Quyon, an old riverside lumbering town, always a mix of both French and English, remains so to this day. It is the site of the ferry crossing to Mohr's Landing, Ontario. Highway No. 148 by-passes this sleepy little town, where singer Lennox Gavan's Hotel has gained its fame — or notoriety — for holding the most rambunctious St. Patrick's Day celebrations in the Valley. However, there are summertime offerings to be found here: a lovely little sandy beach down by the Quyon ferry for a swimming interlude on a really hot day, the home, and the legend, of Granny Bean, and the Mohr House.

Just across from the Catholic church is the tiny, exquisite cottage in which, from 1820 to 1880, Granny Bean kept a stopping-place for shantymen and rivermen back in Quyon's lumbering era. Then, on a summer's day in 1860, she gained a place in history when the Prince of Wales, later Edward VII, made an unscheduled stop at the Quyon docks. Word was sped to Granny that royalty was on the way. Quickly realizing that she was ill prepared, she made the rounds of the monied folk in town — the McCanns, the Brunsons, the Amms, the McLeans, the Mohrs —

GRANNY BEAN'S STOPPING-PLACE, QUYON

Granny Bean ran a stopping-place for rivermen and lumbermen on this site from 1820 to 1880. Her most famous guest was the Prince of Wales, later Edward VII, in 1860.

and in no time at all gathered up borrowed china, silver, and linen "fit for a king."

Quyon boasts another great house that is unique in the Valley: the towering white frame of early lumberman William Mohr. It's set right on the main street in the midst of a stand of white pine, but so well hidden by bush and trees that, in summer, you have to search for it. Fortunately it's being carefully watched by the National Capital Commission and is in the hands of Mohr's descendants, who realize its historical value and treasure it. Mohr's father, John Christian, was an early settler to Onslow Township, taking up his 2,000 acres about 1840.

But Quyon was really the town that grew up around lumberman John Egan's first sawmill and later, after 1846, around his lumber mill near the mouth of the Quyon River, where he had acquired vast timber limits of white pine.

John Egan began his lumbering career in Quyon, spread out to Aylmer and Eganville. Although he died young, he had lived long enough and made such a fortune that envy and resentment against his prosperity and diverse business interests had already channelled itself into anonymous verse. A ballad was even set to music and sung during the provincial election of 1854, when Egan was running for MP for Pontiac."

This is also the town of the legendary wit and storyteller Jim Doherty. Although the "Lad from Ragged Chute," back of Quyon, has been dead for some 25 years, his sense of humour, earthy wit, and quick repartee have left a trail behind him that extends through the Valley from Quyon to Sheenboro on the Quebec side and from Calabogie to Killaloe on the Ontario side.

⁋ STORY

Carl Jennings of Sheenboro told me this one:

One time Jim Doherty was working down at Killaloe. After Mass on Sundays all the Catholics would go out of church and they'd go down to a stable at somebody's farm and they'd all be in there drinking. Father Dowdall with the big white whiskers found them at the barn one day and proceeded to chase them all out. They all scrambled out of the place where they used to shovel the manure out of the stable. And there would always be a shovel left hanging there. Anyway, they all escaped out onto the big pile of manure — except Jim Doherty. He got stuck in the hole there. And Father Dowdall grabbed the manure shovel and started smacking Jim on the ass. And Jim started yelling so hard they could hear him all over both Old and New Killaloe. Jim kept yelling: 'Don't hit so hard, Father! I'm a Protestant! Don't hit so hard, Father, I'm Protestant —' "

✳

Norway Bay

Turn off Highway No. 148 toward the Ottawa River to reach Norway Bay, one of the oldest and formerly most prestigious of the Ottawa area watering places. Today it is becoming a retirement village. One of the first cottagers at this site on the Ottawa was Cushman, superintendent of the E.B. Eddy plant in Hull. Cushman built the beautiful little Cushman memorial church at the waterside which is still used for services for holidayers. At the old dock where the ferryboat across the Ottawa once ran to Sand Point, Ontario, there is public swimming, and you can unpack your picnic lunch at parkside picnic tables here.

Bristol

A short distance farther on Highway No. 148 is the old riverside hamlet of Bristol. Its golf courses are open to both cottagers and tourists. The River View Inn here and the River View Farm at Norway Bay combine to offer campsites, motel units, and housekeeping units as well as sandy swimming beaches, pure maple syrup, fresh honey, and hayrides. The Annual Country Jamboree Weekend in July features old-time fiddling and square dancing.

Shawville

It is no accident that Shawville is the heartland of Anglo-Saxon Protestantism in Western Quebec. When James Pendergast emigrated from Ireland in 1825, he brought his dreams of being surrounded by a settlement without the religious tensions of his homeland. When he became Crown Land Agent, he made one condition: only Protestants would be allowed to settle in his territory.

For many years the scene of one of the country's biggest annual Orangemen's parades and picnics on King Billy's Twelfth of July, it was Shawville that, through its century-old weekly, *The Shawville Equity*, threatened to secede from Quebec during the Quebec Revolt and separatist crisis. When Quebec signs were put up in Shawville a number of years ago, they were very quietly removed in the night — and never put up again.

The main street is lined with great Victorian brick homes (made from local bricks fired at the old Hodgins Brickyard), including Bryan Murray's house (the hockey coach), the Strutt house, the Dr. Wallace Hodgins house, the Hynes house, and the Dr. F.G. Rogers house. The heritage bodies of French-speaking Roman Catholic Quebec are looking very protectively at these splendid houses, for they demonstrate what a very prosperous service centre Shawville once was for the rich and thriving farming community surrounding it. Parts of the Clarendon Inn on the main street go back to 1820.

Shawville is an anomaly in Quebec in another way: it has five Protestant churches, including one of the few remaining Standard or Holy Roller churches in the country. Shawville is the birthplace of Bishop John Horner, founder of the Holiness Movement–Standard Church (Holy Roller) of America. Camp meetings were a very important part of this sect, which was an offshoot of the Methodists. For many years it was Shawville's proudest boast that they didn't have a "Frog" or "Mick" in town. From a 1930 *Government of Quebec Department of Highways and Mines Tourist Guide*: "The Municipality of Shawville, situated on the line of the Canadian Pacific Railway, was founded in 1840 under the name of Saint-Alexandre-de-Clarendon. Several years later this name was replaced by that of Sainte-Melanie and, in 1917, the latter gave place to that of Saint-Jacques-le-Majeur-de-Shawville."

Always a hockey town, Shawville was the birthplace of all-star right winger Frank Finnigan, "The Shawville Express," who played with the old Ottawa Senators in the 1920s and with the Toronto Maple Leafs on the Thoms, Boll, and Finnigan line in the early 1930s. With the death of King Clancy in 1986, Finnigan became the last of the Ottawa Senators.

Started in 1858, the Shawville Fair has remained one of the great fall events of the Ottawa Valley, with the horse show and harness racing always major attractions. The Fair runs the first weekend in September.

Shawville is the home of some of the great storytellers of the past. Indeed, just as Quyon is famous for its fiddlers, Shawville is famous for its storytellers. Phoebe McCord, Dale Thomson, Frank Finnigan, Jr., the late Lou McDowell, and the late Bob Judd are among the best in the Valley — and of course the greatest of all, the late G.A. Howard.

❡ STORY

G.A. Howard was a beloved character and a master of spoonerisms who ran the first Ford dealership in the Valley selling cars with "baboon tires," "automatic cut-offs," "rubber bunters," and "self-commencers."

G.A.'s great wit probably contributed to his becoming very successful with his Ford dealership and he felt he was rich enough to be able to afford a trip to Toronto on the CPR. In those days, as now, there was an underground passage from Toronto Union Station to the big hotels.

As. G.A. strode along in his Sunday suit, a redcap moved up quickly beside him, anxious to serve such an obviously important traveller.

"King Eddy?" the redcap queried.

"No," came the quick reply, "G.A. Howard from Shawville, Quebec."

✳

Shawville Steam Fair

A grass-roots affair drawing people to the Valley from as far away as Niagara and Alberta, the Shawville Steam Fair takes place in the middle of August on Eric Campbell's farm, R.R. No. 1, The Townline, Clarendon. Signs are posted all the way from Highway No. 148. The show features turn-of-the-century steam threshing machines, a horse-drawn vintage steam winch, antique cars, an ice-road snow plow from the old lumber camps, one team pulling and one team pushing. Many of the old machines on display are still "alive," threshing oats and sawing wood. Prizes and trophies are distributed for the best restored steam machines. The club has a permanent collection and is particularly proud of its 20-22 hp Waterloo steam engine, used for a sawmill or threshing mill, donated by the late Arnold Corrigan of Shawville.

SIDE TRIP EAST OF SHAWVILLE

If you follow Highway No. 303, heading east, it will lead you through lovely cottage and resort country, passing through Charteris, Thorne Centre, Schwartz, and Ladysmith up to Otter Lake, an area of Polish and German "pocket" settlements.

❡ STORY

I t was fashionable for royalty and noblemen from England to visit the colonies and tour the Ottawa Valley. In 1872 Prince Arthur, who later became the Duke of Connaught and Governor General of Canada from 1914 to 1918, travelled up the Ottawa to Otter Lake. His hosts were representatives of two of the largest lumber companies in North America, the Gillies Brothers and the Gilmour Brothers. One of the highlights of the Prince's trip was a hunting expedition up the Picanoc River. On their way upriver the royal party stayed at Depot Farm, a stopping-place for lumbermen at Otter Lake. About 12 miles from Otter Lake on the Picanoc Road, a monument has been erected on the site where the Prince is supposed to have cut down a huge tree.

Some of the Gillies and Gilmour shantymen who accompanied the royal party to make the fires, cook the meals, and act as guides were French-speaking lads. According to the legend the Prince was a magical hunter. One time when he aimed at a black duck he shot a white one. The French Canadian shantymen were amused by the Prince's attempts at hunting and they made up a song that has come down to us as *"V'la l'bon vent."*

❋

The Ladysmith Oktoberfest is organized by the German community for the first weekend every October.

The Centre Touristique du Lac Leslie at Otter Lake provides

camping, swimming, and canoeing in a beautiful wilderness setting. At Otter Lake, also, L'Auberge Leslie Ranch Inn is a year-round vacation centre for all ages with a great variety of activities: horseback riding, canoeing, swimming, nature trails, guided tours of the region's hunting and fishing sites, ice fishing, cross-country skiing, skidooing, and nature camping.

Portage-du-Fort

On the western outskirts of Shawville at an overhead flashing light, you come to a turnoff from Highway No. 148 onto No. 301 that takes you to Portage-du-Fort. Next to Aylmer, this is the most historical, scenic, and beautifully situated town on this tour. In fact, it is an ideal town to walk in. Despite the fact that it was half-burned to the ground in 1914, Portage-du-Fort remains a treasure of heritage buildings, including Mr. Amy's Marble House (some of the stone for the building of the Parliament Buildings in Ottawa was quarried here and carted by wagonloads to Ottawa), merchant Reid's stone mansion (it now houses a defunct hotel), a charming yellow Victorian frame (home of Mountain Jack Thomson, legendary giant of the Ottawa Valley), and the stone storage sheds and church left behind by lumberman George Usborne.

At the foot of the main street, on the site of the War Memorial at Harbour Square, the first white scout, young Nicholas Vignau, in 1611 landed with a party of Algonquin Indians en route to their tribal headquarters upriver at Calumet Island. Here they had to portage around a series of five cataracts before reaching a level of the river 100 feet higher above sea level. As Canada's greatest artery of east-west fur trade for more than two centuries, the Ottawa River carried most of the explorers and traders on to the Upper Great Lakes, to the valleys of the Mississippi, to the Mackenzie River, and to all the rivers of the Western plains as well as the shores of the Pacific Ocean north of California. Like the ancient footpath around the Chaudière Rapids at Hull, the portage trail from Harbour Square to Bentley's Landing is one of the oldest footpaths in Canadian history. Champlain fought his way along this portage in 1613 prior to wintering over on Ile aux Allumettes. Around 1670, military engineer Sieur de Coulonge established da fur trade fort at Portage along the upper level. It operated for 50 years during the period of the splendid rivalry between the fur express canoes of the North West Company and the Hudson's Bay Company.

By the turn of the nineteenth century the timber trade was following fast on the heels of the disappearing fur masters. In 1810, Henry Usborne, lumber merchant of Quebec City, obtained from the Government of Lower Canada large reserves of pine forest along the Coulonge River, rights that seem to have given him a land claim in the village of Portage-du-Fort.

For me, the romance of the early Usbornes permeates this town. George Usborne was an English sea captain who came to Quebec City early in the nineteenth century, bought three ships, and began shipping square timber from Quebec to Liverpool. He prospered, built a large stone house at Quebec City, and settled there with his American bride, Mary Seton Ogden. During a storm in the Atlantic, Usborne lost three ships and their cargoes and was forced into bankruptcy. He had to sell out in Quebec City and start anew in the wilderness of the upper Ottawa, where the timber trade was booming. There, he built again in stone, including the lovely little Anglican church on the hillside where he and Mary are buried.

The first steamboat on the Ottawa, the *George Buchanan*, was built in 1836 at Arnprior to portage passenger traffic the length of Chats Lake (Shaw Lake). The boat docked at the Harbour Square wharf in Portage-du-Fort, followed by steamers *Alliance, Oregon*, and *Snowbird*. As passenger service on the river neared the end of its era, to be replaced by roads and motor travel, the Upper Ottawa Improvement Company, (ICO) continued some passenger river service, but their boats, the *Murphy, Hamilton, Opeongo, Robinson*, and *Samson*, were used mostly for towing timber on the Ottawa. Over the years Portage-du-Fort became "the home port" for many of the crewmen, captains, and pilots of the river traffic.

Much of historic interest remains, despite the fire that ravaged Portage-du-Fort — so much, indeed, that one is compelled to wonder what an even greater treasure the village might have been if it were all intact today. The stone buildings include:

- *St. George's Anglican Church*, 1856
- *St. James Roman Catholic Church*, 1850
- The *Pentecostal Church*, formerly the *Presbyterian Church*
- The home of blacksmith *MacDonald*, dating to the 1840s on

Mill Street, now owned by Mrs. Joe Malette

• The *Dr. Purvis Home*, now the *James School*. (Dr. Purvis lies in the village cemetery in a section or plot fenced by wrought-iron work.)

• Notary *S.A. MacKay's Home*, now owned by Mrs. O. Giroux

• Boatman *Joseph Tanguay's Home*, now owned by a family from Ottawa

• Lumber baron George Usborne's *Stone Storage Sheds* on the river

• The *Dr. Gaboury Home* on the top of the hill, later called the *Dagg Farm House*

• The *Town Hall*, 1840s, used as a school long before the brick schoolhouse was built in 1881

• The *St. James Stone Schoolhouse*, later converted into a convent and then a private home

• The *Reid House*, now the *Pontiac Hotel*, the home of general storekeeper Reid.

But perhaps the most interesting survivals of the great fire of 1914 were the frame buildings, the Tanguay store-and-house combination and the house of Mountain Jack Thomson.

After a tour through town, there's a beach for swimming and a shady park for picnicking, all within the sound of the tumult of the Ottawa River as it rushes over the Chenaux Power Dam. On the swimming beach, Lady Head's monument adds a note of humour (she was the first woman to come by canoe up the Ottawa). It's on the reverse side of the town's War Memorial — somebody was saving money.

Bryson and *Calumet Island*

Unless you're brave enough to try to angle your way across country on the back roads, you'll have to retrace your steps a few miles back on Highway No. 301 to No. 148, where you'll turn north again and head toward Bryson. At this juncture, follow the sign to Calumet Island, site of early Algonquin Indian settlements and of two fabled timber slides of the lumbering saga, the Mountain Slides and the Calumet Slides.

Follow the river road through the picturesque village of Calumet with its great stone Catholic church, surveying the Ottawa's gentler side. On the fringes of the village, set on a tiny knoll in the little grove of trees, you'll discover the gleaming white gravestone of Jean Cadieux, one of the legendary heroes of the Valley.

✦ STORY

Cadieux was a Hudson Bay trader who settled on Calumet Island and intermarried with the Algonquins there. One day an Algonquin runner raced into camp crying out that the Iroquois were coming. They had a reputation as ruthless aggressors, so a plan was formulated whereby Cadieux and two braves would act as decoys, leading the enemy into the woods while the rest of the encampment escaped by canoe. The plan was successful to the extent that the canoes escaped. More than that, the legend tells how St. Anne entered the lead canoe and guided the others all the way down to the Lake of Two Mountains. However, Cadieux wrote his famous lament on a piece of birchbark, which is said to have hung for many years at the gravesite. One of the verses reads:

"Fly, nightingale, to the dear ones I'm leaving.
Fly to my wife and my little ones grieving.
Tell them I guarded love and loyalty.
And to abandon any hope of seeing me."

✸

After you've stood a moment on this hallowed ground, you can go back a little way to Au Bouleau Blanc, The White Birch, one of the few recommendable places to eat in the area. Five years ago Mr. and Mrs. Alex Tremblay and their four oldest children began building this stacked cedar-log restaurant overlooking the Ottawa. Downstairs there's a free pool table, and outside are picnic tables and a swimming pool (if you're like I am and don't like pools, Bryson Beach is nearby). Recently a screened-in patio extension was added. The bill of fare isn't extraordinary, the specialty is surf and turf, but if you're lucky you might arrive on a day when fresh fish has been caught. What is extraordinary about Au Bouleau Blanc is its adjoining 182 acres of marked cross-country trails for skiing in the winter and hiking in the summer. As well, "nature" camping is allowed on this huge tract (no facilities).

I particularly recommend exploring the south (mountain) end of Calumet Island, where the views down the Ottawa River are spectacular.

"The Legend of the White Birch"

Today, descendants of the friendly Algonquins still live on Ile du Grand Calumet. Mostly we hear stories of fights and feuds with the Indians. But in actual fact, the early explorers and settlers were dependent on the Indians for help with portage routes, with construction of shelters, with methods of hunting for food, with types of edible plants — anything that would help them survive in the wilderness. Explorer Jacques Cartier found how important the Indians' help was to him when all his men were dying of scurvy from a lack of Vitamin C. Cartier tells us about it:

Dom Agaya, an Indian whom I saw ten or twelve days ago, was extremely ill with the very disease that my men were suffering from; for one of his legs about the knee had swollen to the size of a two-year-old baby, and the sinews had become contracted. His teeth had gone bad and decayed and the gums had rotted and become tainted. I inquired of him what had cured him of his sickness. Dom Agaya replied that he had been healed by the juice of the leaves of a tree and the dregs of this, and that this was the only way to cure sickness. Two squaws with us brought nine or ten branches. They showed us how to grind the bark and the leaves and to boil it whole in water. Of this one should drink every two days and place the dregs on the legs where they were swollen and affected. I at once ordered a drink to be prepared for the sick men. As soon as they had drunk it they felt better. After drinking it two or three times they recovered health and strength and were cured of all the diseases they had ever had."

This Magical Tree, of course was, Le Bouleau Blanc — the White Birch.

*

From the Bryson Bridge Marina, Captain John and Bernice (Gardiner) Brusenbauch run the *Pontiac Princess,* a 20-passenger steel-hulled boat built by Captain John, up the Ottawa on charter cruises, four or eight hours each. Cruise members on the eight-hour cruise leave at 9 A.M. and can have lunch at the Davidson Yacht Club, where there is also an indoor pool and a beach for swimming, or they may choose to pack their own picnics and wine. The shorter cruise leaves at noon. The *Pontiac Princess* operates from May 15 to September 30. At the marina you can rent all kinds of boats, canoes, sailboats, power boats, as well as windsurfing boards. The same company also runs *Calumet Voyageur,* a six-hour rafting trip on the Ottawa.

SIDE TRIP UP HIGHWAY NO. 301

If you are still hungry for more byways in this country, follow Highway No. 148 north a few miles to Campbell's Bay. This secondary, paved, but virtually untravelled highway is simply a feast of mountains that I find incomparable in both the Gatineau and the Opeongo range. I've travelled it in all seasons, and its wide-angle vistas move me to a feeling of belonging to the universe that extends far beyond pantheism. In Campbell's Bay you can take one of the guided trips run by Pontiac Tours, emphasizing the history and folklore of the area.

From there, you can head north on Highway No. 301, to Leslie Lake, where there's a park perfect for picnicking. At nearby Leslie Ranch there's pony riding and horseback riding. Continue along No. 301 to lovely Danford Lake, where there is a very friendly pub if you need a break in the driving. Or continue farther on to Kazabazua (an Indian word meaning "Hidden Currents"), where Highway No. 301 meets No. 105, for a refreshing pause at "the longest bar in the world." There's a pottery-making centre to visit. If you continue east, you'll arrive at Mont Sainte-Marie, a very attractive summer and winter resort. You can have a game of tennis, swim, rent a canoe or a sailboard — all to work up an appetite for the resort's fine cuisine. Reservations are a must for dinner, but not for lunch.

Highway No. 105 will lead you south to Ottawa, if you wish to return at this point, or you can drive back to Campbell's Bay and continue your trip along No. 148.

Fort Coulonge

If you stay on Highway No. 148, you'll head into Fort Coulogne.
I don't need to warn you to slow down as you approach this town.
The brakes will be applied at the sight of a large, barn-red,
covered bridge (the third longest in Quebec) looming up in front
of you and reflected in the waters of the Coulonge River. Fort
Coulonge is imprinted with the former power and influence of
timber baron George Bryson.

You can walk or drive across Bryson's bridge, built to expedite
the movements of his shantymen and supplies. Across the bridge
a short distance up the street you will come to one of the most
beautiful little stone Presbyterian churches in the Valley. Across
from the church, nestled amid tall white pines, sit three magnificent stone houses, built by George Bryson for his three children.
Just past these houses is the little white frame ''child's-drawing''
house, the residence of shantyman Rich Durocher. Before his
death a few years ago he was one of the last of the Gillies men.
Prior to his occupancy, the house was Bryson's Bank, from which
he issued money with his own face on it. Farther down the street
on the right is a large prosaic stone structure, now a school but
originally a Hennessy residence. I like the local legend that goes
with this house.

¶ S T O R Y

The late Fred Davis of Fort Coulonge told me this story:

Seems the Hennessys were making money in lumber and
Martin Hennessy once fought Big Joe Montferrand. One of
the up-and-coming Hennessys married a Bryson, an ill-
considered match in Bryson circles. So, just to prove he was as
good as anyone else, or better, Hennessy built this stone house
bigger than any 'damn Bryson house on the street.' If you look at
Hennessy's stone house carefully, you'll see the house he built to
prove a point proves you can't build a house to prove a point.''

✳

After you retrace your steps to your car, you can either walk or
drive to Bryson's original white neo-classical frame with the
widow's walk, from which he surveyed his thousands of hectares

of farmland and timber stand. The house was saved from demolition through the efforts of a heritage group headed by architectural designer Philip Gabriel of Campbell's Bay. It's now been externally restored and internally renovated (à la Quebec government policy) under the direction of Pierre Cayer, the architect of Hull's Hotel de Ville. Funded by the Municipality of Mansfield and Pontrefact, the building will be used by the Centre Local de Services Communautaires. In August 1988 the Bryson house will be partially open so the public can view the displays that Gabriel was commissioned to design.

Today, descendants of the Algonquins live in Fort Coulonge, some of them still acting as hunting and fishing guides.

¶ STORY

This story is from an interview with Emile Bertrand of Fort Coulonge:

I was in big log jams. One in 1967 on Ragged Chute was 50 or 60 feet high and we were 25 days trying to get it loose — 150 men on it, and bulldozers. Well, when that log jam finally took off along the shores it cut off great big trees — cedar, poplar, pine, no matter what — it took them off at the roots as it roared down.

"And the noise was like a volcano. Three miles away at Jim's Lake the breakup of the log jam made such a noise that a hen broke the eggs under her when she jumped up in the air. And five miles away the cows at Sheenboro quit milking for two days. At Demer's Centre a hundred sheep died of fright."

*

SIDE TRIP TO GRAND CHUTE PARK AND THE PONTREFACT COUNTRY RESORT

Just outside Fort Coulonge, the Bois-Franc Road (locally called the Bufferaw Road in the English bastardization) turns toward the mountains and the tumultuous chutes of the Coulonge River as it tumbles toward the Ottawa. This is an area in the process of development. Le Parc de la Grand Chute has a little snack restaurant, a few picnic tables, about a mile of walking trail, and a new bridge spanning one of the five chutes at this site. A square timber raft is assembled on land here, the same as those made up a hundred years ago by timber baron George Bryson after his 60-foot-long timbers had shot the Bryson slide here, circumventing the grand chute and its spectacular gorge.

Pontrefact Country Resort

Pontrefact is an all-season 600-acre resort in process of development. It offers a beautifully situated 18-hole golf course; 20 miles of cross-country skiing with junior, intermediate, and senior trails; a small lodge with rooms at a modest price or "a presidential suite with fireplace, whirlpool, balcony overlooking the golf course and river"; and a restaurant in the main lodge. From March 15 to April 30 the Pontrefact Maple Sugar Cabin is open. There is taffy on the snow, visits to the Grand Chute in the spring runoff, as well as full-course meals featuring house bread, home-made beans, home fries, sausages, ham, oreilles de crisses, soufflés, pancakes, and sugar pie.

Chapeau

From Fort Coulonge, head north on Highway No. 148 to the turn-off to Chapeau on Allumette Island, the storied seeding ground of famous Canadian folksongs sung by John and Pat Gregg's Chapeau Boys. From the silver-spired hilltop St. Alphonse-Liguori Church (*circa* 1885) to the famous Chapeau Bridge, the lines of the Chapeau Boys echo to this day:

> "Now the boys from Chapeau can dance and can sing;
> Sure they're just as happy as emperor or king.
> We've seven fine fiddlers, there's none of us drones,
> And Michael, me brother, can rattle the bones."

On the main street two historic hotels face each other: Keon's (yes, the proud natives will tell, Wilbert Keon, the world-famous heart surgeon, came from the area) and Meilleur's, for two generations a family-run business, and before that, back to 1852, run by Maloneys and Grays. Hosted by genial giant Freddy Meilleur himself, you enter one of the very last of the small-town hotel dining rooms in the great square-meal tradition.

Whatever you do at Freddy Meilleur's — lunch, dine, drink —

take a little drive through the village of Chapeau and then head over the other bridge across the Ottawa. This bridge is single-lane, so once "you have it," dawdle to look at one glorious view downriver. At the end of the bridge, follow the sign on Highway No. 148 to Chichester–Sheenboro. You are on your way to one of the richest heritage resources in the whole Ottawa Valley: Fort William, site of an original Hudson Bay trading post.

Fort William

Fort William is a place to take off your shoes and walk on sand through history with your children. The site includes the original Hudson Bay factor's house, McCool's brick store with its stone addition where the furs were stored, an Indian mission church, the ruins of an old forge, an Indian burial ground (now almost obliterated), and a vintage hotel set on a wide, pristine sandy beach with a view of the islands of the Ottawa. It's a place for sand walking, picnicking, and swimming unlimited. Or you can drink on the lovely, long, open verandas of the hotel as you watch the pleasure boats enjoy the 45-kilometre stretch of the great Ottawa from The Swisha to Portage.

¶STORY

"A Liar Is Found Out"

When the Indians took their furs to the trading post in Quebec City, Champlain would send back with them French scouts or *coureurs de bois* to gather information for him. On his return to Quebec City, one of these scouts, Nicholas Vignau, told Champlain a wonderful story about reaching a great sea to the north via the Ottawa River. Champlain was very excited, for he felt that Vignau had been to Hudson's Bay and that now there was a route to China by the north. Unfortunately, Vignau had lied to his leader. He had spent the winter comfortably amongst the Algonquins on Allumette Island. The next year when Champlain went up the Ottawa, taking Vignau along with him as his guide, Tessouat, Chief of the Algonquins, told the truth about Vignau's so-called 'explorations.' "

✳

FORT WILLIAM HOTEL

Fort William is the site of a former Hudson Bay post. The hotel is set on a sandy beach with a clear view of the islands of the river from the veranda.

Sheenboro

A short drive beyond Fort William takes you to Sheenboro, the centre of a formerly rich farming community and an almost 100 percent Irish enclave. Sheenboro is renowned for its great storytellers — Carl Jennings, Edwin Doyle, and J.R. Brennan — and noted for the "only underground Catholic church" in the country (it's "underground" because only the first floor was finished) and for its ancient watering hole, Keon's Hotel. There isn't much left of the hamlet since the hotel burned down. But back of Sheenboro at the foot of the mountains lies some of the most beautiful lake country ever created.

Edwin Doyle raises rare Norwegian Fjord horses here and his neighbours, the Brennans, run Brennan's Recreational Farms. Camp rentals on a scenic mountaintop are available, as well as mountain climbing and hiking on Brennan's Bluff, boating and fishing in many lakes on the huge farm complex, horseback riding and a tent and trailer camping ground. Brennan's Harvest Ball is held annually during the July 1 holiday weekend.

¶ STORY

This is another Carl Jennings story:

There was always a great blessing of the seed at Sheen in the springtime. Bushels of seed grain and seed potatoes were taken to the Sheen church and blessed on Rogation Day. But one year Christie Tallon put his bags of blessed seed up over the fansill sieves and forgot about them. He forgot entirely where he had put them, so he had to go ahead and put unblessed seed in his fields. Come fall, all the men were at Keon's Bar in Sheen talking abut the harvest, and Christie said, 'Sure, I can't explain it at all. The best crops I ever had in me life. And all unblessed seed!' "

*

From the Fort William–Sheenboro area the world drops off into wilderness, accessible only by the huge lumber tractor-trailers bringing timber out or by four-wheel-drive vehicles headed into the sequestered hunting and fishing camps.

DIRECTIONS

You can retrace your route to Ottawa along Highway No. 148, or you can drive back as far as Chapeau and, at the southern end of Allumette Island, cross over the bridge that leads to Pembroke on the Ontario side of the river. From there, Highway No. 17 will take you back to Ottawa. From Pembroke, you can commence a tour of the white-water country (Chapter 8) or drive to Renfrew and begin the tour described in the next chapter.

Chapter 6

AROUND
AND ABOUT
RENFREW

Preamble

Dotted with crossroads, hamlets, and waterside villages set against a backdrop of rivers, lakes, and wilderness, Renfrew County might be said to offer "something for everyone": Story-land for the moppets; beaches, music festivals, nightlife for the teenagers; 110 miles of a breathtakingly scenic paradise on the Ottawa River for the boaters; caves for the spelunkers; excellent hunting and fishing for the sportsmen; considerable challenge for both the downhill and the cross-country skiers; museums and antique shops for the history buffs; and restaurants, inns, campsites, motels, hotels, and bed and breakfasts to suit every taste and pocketbook.

The three main towns — Arnprior, Renfrew, and Pembroke — all have lumbering backgrounds and are greatly enhanced by residuals of this nineteenth-century saga of romance and adventure, by old mill sites, and by the many "castles" built by the timber barons. Throughout the countryside are scattered the remainders of the lumbering trade: old lumbering roads, timber

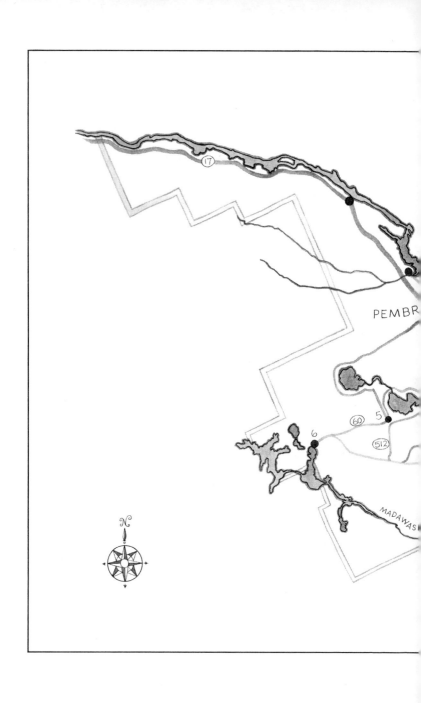

17

PEMBR

60 5

512

6

MADAWAS

N

1 DEEP RIVER
2 COBDEN
3 CALABOGIE
4 EGANVILLE
5 KILLALOE
6 BARRY'S BAY
7 GRIFFITH
8 CASTLEFORD
9 BRAESIDE
10 SANDPOINT
11 WHITE LAKE
12 WABA
13 BURNSTOWN
14 DOUGLAS
15 DACRE

slides, lumber camp ruins, river driver's graves, shantymen's stopping-places.

Renfrew County is one of the entrances to Algonquin Park with its 7,000 square kilometres of wilderness and 1,500 kilometres of canoe routes for nature lovers and adventurers. From Farrell's Landing on the Ottawa below Renfrew to Bark Lake on the fringes of Algonquin Park, meandering through the Opeongo Hills is the fabled Opeongo Line, an 1840 settlers' trail today comprising one of the richest heritage resources on the North American continent, perhaps in the entire world. The Ottawa Valley is reputed to have the largest number of log buildings extant anywhere and Renfrew County is particularly blessed with these national icons. Everywhere you look these *first* log buildings built by our *first* settlers from the *first* trees on the land add an indelible sense of history to the Renfrew County landscape.

PREPARATIONS

Dining and wining is no problem; there are many choices ranging from "ordinary Canadian" to the exclusive Wingle Inn, nestled in the hills above Palmer Rapids, or the Siberia Inn, hidden in the hills at Barry's Bay. There are countless park and picnic sites, many of them on the water, as well as places to swim. So you can pack your picnic and your swimming togs.

You can pick up maps and tourist brochures to Renfrew County at travel booths in Deep River, Pembroke, Cobden, Renfrew, Calabogie, Eganville, Killaloe, Barry's Bay, Arnprior, and Griffith. Study the maps and chart your routes, picking out the places you want to visit. But Renfrew County, like Glengarry County, is well enough populated that, without any real problems to speak of, you can meander any which way, picking and choosing the places of particular interest to you, whether you want to tour all the antique shops in the county, visit the caves at Douglas, or just explore the back roads and byways, stopping wherever your fancy beckons.

Arnprior

Take the Queensway and Highway No. 17 north from Ottawa to Arnprior, at the southernmost tip of Renfrew County. This community has become almost a dormitory town for Ottawa commuters.

HISTORY

If you're talking to a Scot, it was the Scotsmen Archibald Stewart, Duncan Campbell, an old Glengarry soldier, and the Goodwins who were already settled down on the banks of the mighty Madawaska River when the Last Laird MacNab arrived in Arnprior in 1823. If you're talking to an Irishman like John McGonigal of Arnprior, he will tell you that his McGonigal ancestors settled Arnprior. The McGonigals, amongst those "big" Irishmen impressed in Ireland to work with the British naval ratings in Canada, were given land in return for their services.

Arnprior was put on the North American map in the nineteenth century by its two great lumber companies, the McLachlins and the Gillies. Except for a tiny little brick smokehouse, located on the commercial strip at the bridge going over the Madawaska River, where the millworkers were allowed to have a smoke break of ten minutes, nothing remains of the 187-acre site that made up the McLachlin Brothers' lumberyards at the junction of the Madawaska and the Ottawa rivers. And at Braeside, on the River Road just outside Arnprior, a very shrunken Gillies lumber mill site now belongs to the Upper Ottawa Improvement Company (ICO).

WALKING TOUR OF ARNPRIOR

Although the town has not had the good sense yet to "declare" the preservation of its historical sites and rare buildings and subsequently is in the process losing them, it remains in the old centre part, particularly in the area around the Arnprior Museum, a fascinating town for a walking tour. This section is dotted with

McLachlin dynasty houses, usually great Victorian bricks. Arnprior District and Memorial Hospital on John Street was built around timber baron Dan McLachlin's first stone mansion.

Inch Buie Cemetery, McLachlin Estate, Gillies Estate, the Old Dock

A walk down John Street from Madawaska Street will yield the curious traveller access to four landmark sites that embody the lumbering saga of the Valley — Inch Buie Cemetery (a history lesson in itself), the McLachlin Estate, the Gillies Estate, and the Old Dock.

Inch Buie Cemetery, on the riverside at the foot of John Street, is one of the oldest cemeteries in the country and the final haven of many of the famous, near-famous, and infamous of the Valley. The land for the cemetery was given to the town of Arnprior by no less than the Last Laird MacNab at a time when he lived nearby in Kinnell Lodge, now the site of the McLachlin Estate. Buried in the cemetery is one of MacNab's old friends, timber baron Alexander Macdonell, King of the Four Rivers, who built his empire just outside Arnprior at Sand Point. The Macdonnell family plot is unmistakable, ringed as it is by a beautiful, low, wrought-iron fence. Nearby are the McLachlin dynasty burial obelisks, made at the Marble Works in Arnprior and sometimes soaring 20 feet into the air. One of the McLachlin governesses is buried in the family plot.

Just across the park from the cemetery is the gatekeeper's house for the McLachlins, a tiny well-preserved frame cottage inside the iron gates. If you look down the long, winding lane with its great white pine towering over it, you can see your heritage and your children's heritage: the stone residence of the First Dan McLachlin. Unfortunately for travellers, both the McLachlin Estate and the Gillies Estate have been made into Roman Catholic religious institutions and closed off to the public. Still, you can glimpse the grandeur of those early times and sense the presence of the Valley timber barons at these sites.

The Old Dock at the end of John Street, a local swimming hole for the young folk of the town, is ghosted by the legendary John T. Waite, one of the Valley's first homeopaths and a memorable character.

Now John T. Waite was a very religious and very good-living man. No one in Arnprior could ever say a word against his character. For many months he had said he was prepared to show that man, by faith, could walk on water. All his friends and relatives kept at him constantly until he came to the point where he had to prove that man, by faith, could walk on water. So a certain Sunday morning was set and the site was chosen, the old wooden wharf on the Ottawa at the foot of John Street. The whole town of Arnprior was gathered to watch a miracle on the Ottawa. And John T. Waite went down that Sunday morning and walked off the end of the wharf into the Ottawa River and, of course, disappeared.

"When he emerged, he wasn't nonplussed. He simply waved to the crowd of onlookers and pronounced, 'The faith of John T. Waite wasn't strong enough, as you can see . . .' "

✳

Now go back up John Street and walk west until you come to a dead end margined by a white picket fence and a white picket gateway with two Grecian lamps — in wood, of course — on the gateposts. This is one entrance to the "dark Druidical groves" of the Gillies Estate, encompassing another historical landmark.

The completely hidden New England-style white frame mansion, constructed during the Depression years for David Gillies, was built of every kind of beautiful wood the timber baron could desire and his lumbering world could provide. Past the dense woods, which act as bastion to this "castle," Gillies planted all kinds of rare imported trees on the grounds immediately surrounding the house. When Mrs. D.A. Gillies was alive, townsfolk could amble or jog through this enchanted forest. On her death, the estate was willed to the United Church of Canada, to which the Gillies had given generous and staunch support. When the United Church refused the bequest, federal government officials seriously considered this arboreal treasure as a site for a forestry school. It was also thought of as a possible new summer home for the Governor General of Canada. In the end the estate was purchased by the Roman Catholic Church.

How dearly this land was held in the hearts of some Arnprior-

ites is demonstrated by a letter to the editor of *Ontario Magazine*,
June, 1981:

> "Having grown up in Arnprior only two blocks from the
> Gillies property I spent a good deal of my childhood under
> those white pines. . . . The Gillies estate should be experienced
> for years to come by anyone who wants to see what the forests
> of the Ottawa Valley were like when Champlain and the Jesuit
> missionaries came down the Ottawa river over 350 years ago.
>
> "If the historic Gillies house or the equally historic proper-
> ty is let fall into the hands of developers or a private individual
> who, unlike Mrs. Gillies, won't allow public access to the
> place, I think it would be disastrous not only for the town of
> Arnprior but the country too."

The Arnprior Museum

During his lifetime D.A. Gillies was instrumental, along with
other townsfolk, in saving the old Town Hall, at the corner of John
and Madawaska streets, to be used as a library-museum combination. As might be expected, the museum is liberally endowed with
memorabilia, photographs, and tools of the lumbering trade. As
well, it has been presented with a rare antique collection of skates.

The Old Madawaska Hotel

Arnprior was the birthplace and is now the home of storyteller
and songwriter, Bernie Bedore, renowned as the creator of the
Tall Tales of Joe Mufferaw. Bedore dubbed this part of the country
"Big Pine Country." Now in his sixties, he developed his ear for
storytelling back in the 1920s and 1930s. As a young boy Bedore
sometimes worked in the old Madawaska Hotel, then owned by
his father. The lobby was filled with old shantymen, retired from
McLachlin and Gillies, many of them living out their lives on their
savings, paying for room and board in the "old Madawasky."
Bedore's rich repertoire comes from his early childhood, when he
listened to these great old characters entertaining each other and
passing the time with tall tales, old songs, and legends from their
past on the rivers and in the bush.

ARNPRIOR TOWN HALL

The Arnprior Town Hall houses a combined library-museum featuring tools of the lumbering trade and a rare collection of ice skates. Lumberman D.A. Gillies was instrumental in saving this heritage building.

❧ STORY

This story came from Tony Sloan of Ottawa:

S hanty Jack Gilchrist was the father of Donny Gilchrist, the late lamented champion step-dancer. Shanty Jack worked in the Gillies lumber camps where, of course, no liquor was allowed because the evil spirits would precipitate fights, injuries, and time lost off work. Gillies had also just banned butter in all the camps — it was too expensive — and the men were very angry about this deprivation in a diet that was already below par, comprised as it was of sweet pork and beans.

"One day Shanty Jack was standing by when Gillies came in to inspect the camp.

" 'Do I smell whisky here?' Gillies roared out.

" 'Well,' snapped Shanty Jack, 'you sure as hell don't smell butter.' "

❋

Kevin's Antiques and Art

Also on Madawaska Street you may like to amble into Kevin's Antiques and Art to get a further sense of the Arnprior area. They stock Ottawa Valley primitive pine, wicker, oak, and ash furniture as well as hand-painted glass and china. They sell furniture "in the rough" and paintings of local scenes by Kevin Dodds.

The Valley Carver

Ten miles out of Arnprior on the River Road is the Valley Carver, the studio and sales outlet of wood carver Delbert Jubé. The River Road is the scenic route to Renfrew, Castleford, Braeside, and Sand Point. It is rich in Ottawa Valley log buildings, offering some spectacular views of the Ottawa River.

Around and About

Waba and *White Lake*

These little towns back of Arnprior and Renfrew (west on Highway No. 2) provide charming milieus for meandering, for leisurely flea-picking, shopping, walking, antiquing, picnicking, snacking, wining, exploring. As well, the area is filled with the hidden-away studios of artists, artisans, and craftsmen, some of them internationally known.

The area around Waba and White Lake is known as "Feud Country." And not without historical basis. In 1823 the Last Laird MacNab, having been drummed out of Scotland for nonpayment of his debts, fled to Canada, settling first in the Arnprior area. On the site of the present McLachlin mansion, now in possession of the Oblate Fathers, MacNab with impressed settler labour built his first huge log chieftain dwelling, called Kinnell Lodge. When MacNab obtained from the Family Compact a land grant of 81,000 acres, he immediately imported settlers from his native Highland country and proceeded to set up an old-fashioned feudal system, oppressing his clansmen-settlers, extracting annual tithes from them, as well as refusing to allow them to cut his timberlands. Sporadic rebellions on the settlers' part eventually led to the expulsion of NacNab in 1840. But a sense of the 20-year feud between Archibald MacNab and his settlers still permeates the area 150 years later. Some of these oppressed settlers' graves can be seen in the old Flat Rapid Cemetery; in the White Lake Cemetery markers remain for the graves of MacNab's "companion," Catherine "Granny" Fisher; his son, Allan Dhu; and mill owner John Paris. Paris was one of the men who rebelled against MacNab's tyranny, and although his little white frame house passed out of the Paris family's hands just a few years ago, it still stands well preserved in Waba today.

Situated on a very large lake by the same name, the village designated a waterside site as a park. It provides good swimming and boating, and there are wayside picnic tables as well as a public boat-launching ramp.

149

The late Alec McDermid told me this story:

Yes, my great-grandfather John McDermid came out with MacNab in 1823, signed that terrible contract [with him], and then killed himself working trying to fulfill the MacNab's conditions. My great-grandfather was in the gang that went to Arnprior to kill MacNab. There was a leak and the Old Chief was gone when they got there.

"The country was always full of MacNab stories. My brother told me one time about listening to some very old women who had known the Chief talk about him, reminiscing as it were.

"And one old lady said: 'Ah, the Chief, he was a great man for his dancing.'

"And the second old girl said: 'Ah, the Chief, he was a great man for his drinking.'

"And the third old girl said: 'Aye, yes to all that, but he was a great man for his "riding." '

"They still say here in MacNab country that the settlers blew their horns so that people along the way would know that the MacNab and his son, Allan Dhu, were coming. Then the women had to hide . . .

"And speaking of dancing, one old lady said that MacNab often had the pipers out on the green in front of the house at White Lake [now the museum] and the Old Chief and his lady, Catherine Fisher, they were all dancing all night on the green, all dancing on the green in the moonlight . . ."

✳

Waba Cottage Museum

Situated in the lakeside park, the Waba Cottage Museum site includes S.S. No. 53, an old Lochwinnoch school, a little church moved from Sand Point, as well as restored Waba Cottage, the second residence of the Last Laird MacNab and now a museum housing MacNab and family memorabilia.

A female Box descendant of the Last Laird inherited Waba Cottage from the MacNab estate. But in 1939, weary of souvenir seekers and trespassers, she put a bomb to it. Recognizing its historical significance in 1962, an Arnprior heritage group restored

Waba Cottage from its bombed-out ruins. The grey stone at the base of the building today comprises the original remains; the golden stone is new.

❡ STORY

Johnny Campbell of White Lake is one of the few living people who can still speak with authenticity in the oral tradition about his memories, observations, and feelings surrounding the story of the Last Laird MacNab. He tells this amusing story of the White Lake settlement:

This land, which belongs to my family and has for generations, was taken up in 1845 by Alexander Stewart, known as Snappy Sandy. The Stewarts around here were divided into two groups: the Churchfield Stewarts — they were tee-totallers and they built the first church in Renfrew County — and then there were the Drinking Stewarts. Well, one time Church-field John Stewart decided he wanted to build a cedar-log barn, 35-by-50 feet. Well, the local building experts said it couldn't be done and they stood around and laughed while Churchfield John Stewart erected his barn. It's there to this day."

✻

On the main street of White Lake, in a charming century-old building, the Images Gallery features paintings by resident artists Valerie Roos and John Webster, as well as a distinctive collection of contemporary Canadian crafts.

If you take the turn south at the crossroads in town you will come to another interesting craft centre on the notorious Bellamy Road. An ancient local ditty goes:

"White Lake for Whisky
and The Bellamy Road for fun."

In a restored log house Anita Hamilton of Hamilton Pottery makes a wide selection of functional ceramics. She works mostly in porcelain and decorates by brush in an assortment of colour-ful glazes. Dinnerware is a specialty and orders for personal dinnerware are accepted.

Burnstown

Continue on secondary Highway No. 2 through Waba and White Lake to Burnstown. Sensitive and responsible restoration in this picturesque little town on the banks of the Madawaska River virtually transforms it into a mini-Upper Canada Village. The town includes a brick church, a general store, restored log buildings, heritage houses, an old brick school, and Leckie's Hotel, one of the most historic stopping-places in the country. The diversity and talents of its inhabitants make Burnstown a hive of creative and commercial activity.

Over the past 15 years Tim and Diane Gordon have painstakingly restored the *Burnstown General Store*, a large spread of adjoining brick and log sections built at different times over the years. The Robertsons, first settlers, built the log section in 1829, when the Last Laird MacNab was very much part of the scene. In 1879 store owner Robertson added the brick sections.

The Gordons have retained all the nineteenth-century store furnishings and fixtures. They sell crafts, "general store things," scooped ice cream, and baked goods from the local women; the store is also central to the whole countryside for the purchase of Canadiana books. The log wing features continuous local art shows.

To the south across the road from the Burnstown General Store in the old brick schoolhouse, Graham Ditchfield and his staff of experts do furniture restoration, Victorian millwork and screen doors, horse-drawn vehicle restoration, reproduction furniture and door systems; there is also a selection of Canadian and British antiques, including European stained-glass pieces, for sale. A little walk up the main street brings you to *Country Classic*; housed in a restored blue-and-white frame store and run by Paul Delong, it features Canadiana. (If you are lucky during the summertime you may arrive on one of the days when the young merchants of Burnstown have decided to have a sidewalk sale or a flea market.)

On the northwest corner of the crossroads in Burnstown, amidst a complex of restored log buildings, sits *Leckie's Hotel*, now the "Fog Run" studio of internationally renowned potter Richard Gill. Here settlers from White Lake held secret meetings to plan the overthrow of the Last Laird MacNab and some of them probably plotted to kill him. It is told in the area that MacNab always carried a C-note ($100 bill) to pay for his lodgings

LECKIE'S HOTEL, BURNSTOWN

Leckie's Hotel is rich with Ottawa Valley history. Settlers held meetings in the hotel to plot the overthrow of the Last Laird McNab. The great lumbermen and rivermen of the 19th century all stopped at Leckie's to kick up their heels.

wherever he went in the Valley. He thought it very amusing that no one could possibly change such a huge amount, and so he always got off without having to pay. Perhaps he tried this trick at Leckie's as well.

In the early days the bar was closed by dropping a boom (it is rumoured to be still intact inside). During the nineteenth-century lumbering era no doubt the bar and the rooms of Leckie's Hotel resounded to the caulk boots and the roars of all the great Valley lumbermen and shantymen — Gentleman Paddy Dillon or Arnprior, Mountain Jack Thomson of Portage-du-Fort, the Frost Brothers of Pembroke, timber king Alexander Macdonell of Sand Point, Cockeye George McKee of Arnprior, giant Martin Hennessy of Pembroke, Joseph Montferrand of Montreal.

Calabogie

At Burnstown, take Highway No. 508 to Calabogie. Most young people today believe that Calabogie was put on the map by the internationally famous National Film Board Film, *The Best Damn Fiddler from Calabogie to Kaladar*, filmed in both the village and the area in 1969, using local Charbonneau children as part of the cast, with stars Kate Reid and Chris Wiggins.

But long before that, Calabogie was a fabled five-hotel roistering lumbering centre on the Madawaska, first stop after Palmer Rapids, "where the Drive began," a mystical place that people constantly talked about and imagined, but had never seen. At home in Ottawa when my mother put on her good hat we always knew she was going out and leaving us. "Where are you going, Mother?" we would clamour.

And she would stick in her hatpin and say with a sly grin, "Oh, I'm off to Calabogie." To this day I think she answered that way because she had heard her father and her brothers, home from the lumber camps, talk about Calabogie in such a way that it was implanted in her imagination as a fanciful, unobtainable place, cloaked in mystery.

Indeed, throughout the whole Ottawa Valley the name Calabogie seems to have always conjured up something legendary and intriguing.

❡ S T O R Y

Carl Jennings told me this story:

Calabogie was a faraway place we always used to hear about here on this side of the river in Sheenboro, Quebec. People used to say, 'Blue skies over Calabogie' and 'Calabogie, where the birds all fly backwards,' and nowadays I hear them say, 'Bogie, Bogie, where everybody's on the pogey.' Anyhow, we always used to think of it as a special place. But we heard it was rough, stony, very hilly land. And I remember my father, Big Bill Jennings, saying that there was this fellow back there in Calabogie started to dig a well in a hillside. He dug and dug for three weeks — and then he fell out of it."

✳

Calabogie proper and the area around Calabogie Lake have become an all-season tourist mecca, with fine dining places, lodges, boat-launching ramps and marinas, swimming and picnicking places, and a golf course. In winter the area becomes a skiing centre, with *Calabogie Peaks* resort providing four T-bars, a chair lift, 16 runs, night skiing, hotel, bar, restaurant, and overnight accommodation. Further area skiing is provided at Candiac (Dacre) and Pakenham.

Today Calabogie has been stripped of many of its heritage buildings, including its five old hotels, but a few, such as *Collins Bed and Breakfast* (the old Box house), the little White church on the water, Billy Dodge's old general store, and the beautifully restored railway station (now an antique store), remain in the village to give the visitor some sense of Calabogie's pioneer days. And certainly the area around the village abounds in those priceless reminders of the nineteenth century — the log houses, barns, and outbuildings that give the countryside such character.

Calabogie Lake (it really is only a widening of the Madawaska River) was once the watering place of two of Renfrew's magnates, M.J. O'Brien, whose fortune was accrued from a combination of lumbering, mining, and railway building, and George Barnett, descendant of the Renfrew lumbering dynasty. These two tycoons shared the whole lake, which today hosts hundreds of cottagers, boaters, visitors, wind surfers, fishermen, and year-round residents.

For a number of years now the social centre of the town has been the *Whippletree Shanty*, the forerunner of all tourist attractions in Calabogie, pioneered by Bill and Prim Blair. The Whippletree features a dining room, a bar and, in the summertime, an open-air patio overlooking Calabogie Lake, with live entertainment and food of your choice cooked to your taste on the barbecues outside. Built of square timbers brought in by the owners from the area, and designed by themselves, the Whippletree Shanty creates an ambiance totally suitable to the lumbering motif of the village. It is a popular destination for bus tours from Ottawa.

In the village itself, competition to the Whippletree Shanty arrived when two wonderfully eccentric motorcycling ladies in their forties, Kathleen Fex and Lise Sculland, decided to restore an old frame residence, almost falling down, in the heart of Calabogie. They opened *Weazy Widgets Gifts and Tea Room* and there they created an easygoing, friendly atmosphere featuring country cooking and home baking. It's a place for a great breakfast with homemade whole wheat toast and muffins hot from the oven. The craft shop, which features folk art from the surrounding area, invites browsing.

Drive past the Whippletree and the white church and *Collins Bed and Breakfast* to a point where, at the turn of the road, you'll come to a historical octagon-shaped building, once the lookout for the overseer for the Houghton lumbering company. From its eight-sided-window range he could see up- and downriver, keeping a careful watch on his workers. Today, artist Sheila Fletcher runs the *Octagon Gallery* there, featuring local water-colour artists as well as exhibitions by guest artists.

❡ STORY

I heard this one from the late Carl Bailey of Calabogie:

Calabogie was a wild place; it always was. It was terrible during the drives and, I think, even after they were over. It was the damnedest place for fights that ever was. I've seen them douse the lights at a dance and cut it off and close it down so that nobody would get killed. I've seen them drinking inside the hall — and outside the hall. Then they started the police coming and staying right in the hall. . . .

"Back then the country was full of fightin' men. I've heard of the Horners of Pontiac County, real fightin' men. I have known of fellows that would take a dislike for each other — for good. The Klosses and the Lalondes, they fought every time they met; you could class it as a feud.

"And I've heard about Rory Macdonald. I don't know who done it, but he got both eyes gouged out in a fight near Dacre. Men talked about that — it was a terrible thing, you know."

✳

Around the corner, up the hill, past the liquor store, you come to *Calabogie Lodge*, now a dining, fishing, boating, swimming resort, but originally the summer cottage of George Barnett, who was also, by the way, a manufacturer of refrigerators — of which two hefty 1907 wooden originals function to this day in the lodge's bar. The Barnetts, along with M.J. O'Brien, were also amongst the backers of the world-famous Renfrew Millionaires hockey team. Amongst that elite it was common to bet $5,000 on a game and go to Europe for house furnishings.

The Annex, a two-storey house near the lodge, was built for Barnett's longtime caretaker, Neil Campbell, whose children and grandchildren live in Calabogie to this day.

M.J. O'Brien's farm site and summer residence has become *Calabogie Highlands*. There in the summer gazebo above the old boathouse you will perhaps recognize the setting for some of the "love scenes" in *The Best Damn Fiddler from Calabogie to Kaladar*. The whole locale was largely used by director Peter Pearson, whose crew and cast stayed in O'Brien's old cottage, owned by Major Fred Fleming, while shooting was going on. For years afterward, Major Fleming reported that many of his American guests would ask him, "Is this really the place where they shot *The Best Damn Fiddler from Calabogie to Kaladar*?" Major Fleming felt that the film put him on the map, and certainly today his son runs Calabogie Highlands as one of the major lodge accommodation centres in the Valley, featuring an 18-hole golf course.

Barryvale Lodge completes the triumvirate of lodges on Calabogie Lake. It was once a tiny cottage built on the lake about a hundred years ago, but a wealthy American named Gowdy expanded it into a lavish summer home. Now it is a rustic down-home guest house, with an emphasis on food and comfort.

Renfrew

From Calabogie, return along Highway No. 508 to Burnstown, then take No. 2 north to Renfrew.

Locally known as "The Frew," Renfrew, on the banks of the Bonnechere River, began, like most of the permanent settlements of the Valley, in the lumbering trade. In 1830 or so, Lieutenant Christopher James Bell of Castleford on the Ottawa built timber slides to expedite his lumber at the Second Chute of Bonnechere, where Renfrew stands today. Other early developers were politician Sir Francis Hincks and Hudson Bay factor John Lorne McDougall, who logically opened the first store. A lumber jobber named Coyne cleared some land in the area, followed by Joseph Brunette and Thomas McLean. Henry Airth, weary of life under the domination of the Last Laird MacNab, moved to the area. Entrepreneur Xavier Plaunt promoted the business section by selling land cheaply and donating some of it for public buildings. From 1850 on, there was a steady growth in population, mainly Scottish. Many of them walked up the Opeongo Line from the Ottawa River at Castleford.

First a service-centre town for the lumbering trade and later a service-centre town for the farming community, the town remains a major Renfrew County service centre based on a few local industries. It is far enough from Ottawa so as to not lose its character and its local economy in the insidious process of being swallowed up as a commuter town for the Capital City.

Renfrew's leading lumbering families included Martin Russell, the Carswells, the Mackays, the Bannermans, and the Barnetts.

Alexander Barnett sailed to Canada in 1840 and settled back of Renfrew at a little place called Ashdad. There he attempted to set up a feudal system like MacNab's, bringing out settlers from both Ireland and Poland. When this plan failed, he saved $300 from working in the woods as a shantyman, bought a good pair of horses, and began his own lumber company. His timber stands were largely on the Bonnechere, Madawaska, and Petawawa rivers, but eventually the family holdings stretched to British Columbia. The

Barnetts became high-livers, importing their furniture from England and Europe, building large "castles" in keeping with their station, breeding and raising horses that were renowned internationally. Betimes the Barnetts took two carloads of horses to show at the Royal Winter Fair in Toronto. M.J. O'Brien was another one of Renfrew's Horatio Algers, but perhaps the most illustrious expatriate of Renfrew would be Charlotte Whitton, four-term mayor of Ottawa, first lady mayor in Canada, pioneering social worker, lecturer, columnist, and author of *A Hundred Years A 'Fellin'* (a history of the Gillies Company).

❡ STORY

A t Renfrew on Highway No. 17, Pinnacle Hill is a famous landmark, a high and abrupt outcropping in the landscape from which one can see for miles out over the Ottawa Valley. Back in the 1920s in Charlotte Whitton's youth, Pinnacle Hill was a favourite spot for the young people of the Renfrew area to picnic and gambol, park and spark. In 1982 at Renfrew I taped a former classmate of Charlotte Whitton's, the late Mrs. E. Zimmerman, then aged 93, who told of a time she had shared a picnic with a group of young people, including the inimitable Charlotte:

"Even back then Charlotte was beginning to show her true character and high ambitions. I remember her climbing to the very top of Pinnacle Hill high above the rest of us and there pretending to be a great orator, flinging her arms up and shouting out over the whole Ottawa Valley, 'Listen to me! I am Demosthenes!' "

✳

WALKING TOUR OF RAGLAN STREET

Raglan Street, the main street of Renfrew, winds through the entire town, taking you past Butson's landmark motel, past the McDougall Mill, past one of the few remaining original blacksmith's shops on the corner of Raglan Street, through the entire business section, and out onto Renfrew's prime residential area, once the site of two Barnett mansions (only one left), and the house of Judge James Craig, first judge in the Yukon.

McDougall Mill Museum

You will want to visit the McDougall Mill Museum on the Bonne-chere River, just off Raglan Street on Arthur Avenue, in parkland donated by M.J. O'Brien. Picnic tables are located by the rush of the waters, and the site is enhanced by a nearby swinging bridge. Its plaque, put in place by the town's Lionettes, reads: "In memory of the W.H. Kearney family who erected the first swinging bridge here in 1895."

A rare drywall stone construction, the museum building was erected as a grist mill in 1855 by an early politician, fur trader, and merchant, John Lorne McDougall. The three floors of exhibits include early pioneer tools and farm machinery, a military section, a Victorian costume section, a doll and toy exhibit, and personal items belonging to Renfrew-born Charlotte Whitton.

The Upstairs Gallery and Craft Shop

Well worth the long climb up, this Upstairs Gallery and Craft shop is one of the longest-established in the area and the owner's experience shows in the quality and diversity of the merchandise. The gallery features continuous shows by local artists and attracts buyers from Ottawa and Toronto.

The Old Town Hall Tea Room

Although Renfrew has declared its heritage buildings, it doesn't seem to have made much difference. A couple of years ago the primary Barnett mansion on Raglan Street, Coleraine, reputed to have a fireplace in every room, each imported from a different country in the world, was torn down overnight by a developer, and the town almost lost Tommy Barnett's large residence up the street by renting it to a "private boys' school," which used the lumber from the priceless old stables for firewood. In 1988, despite the fact that Renfrew had declared its heritage buildings, Tom Low's White House on Raglan Street, one of the showplaces of the Ottawa Valley, was summarily destroyed to make way for a parking lot.

However, Renfrew has put its abandoned old Town Hall to good use as a tea room. This is a good place to stop on your walking tour with your family, for here you can eat nutritionally and inexpensively, picking and choosing from a menu that includes

TOMMY BARNETT'S HOUSE, RENFREW

Located on Raglan Street, the Tommy Barnett House is a typical Renfrew mansion. Barnett's primary residence, Coleraine, with a specially designed fireplace in every room, was recently destroyed to make way for a modern development.

muffins, sandwiches, homemade soup, quiches, casseroles, salads, and fancy desserts. Traditional afternoon tea — or, if you prefer, coffee — is served with scones and tea biscuits.

The O'Brien Theatre

If you want to get in out of the rain or the heat with your family while you are on tour or on holidays, do as my family and I were so often wont to do: slip into the O'Brien Theatre on Raglan Street for a good movie. Although a small-town movie house, the O'Brien Theatre seems to be run by people who want to provide the community with good theatre fare. Often they get the very latest quality movies on one- or two-night stands on their way through the Valley for the first time.

Renfrew Fair

Begun in 1853, the Renfrew Fair has maintained its reputation as one of the greatest in the whole Ottawa Valley. It takes place the first Wednesday through to the following Monday in September, six days inclusive, on the fairgrounds in the heart of the town, on Highway No. 132, turning off at Coumbes Lane. In 1887 the Renfrew Fair became the first to be electrically illuminated. It is famous for its horse show and horse draws, but is exceptional in all of its classes and divisions.

¶ STORY

This came from an open-line radio program:

A long time ago when the Renfrew Fair was on there was always a bunch of Irishmen who came down from the Mountain [Mount St. Patrick] to go to the fair. This story was passed on to me by my father and he was 92 when he died, so it was a long time ago. In those early days the women used to get into it, too — it wasn't just the men that got into the fights — and they didn't wear silk stockings. They wore the woollen ones and they used to fill them with gravel and then they used them as bludgeons in the fights. Anyway, one time at the Renfrew Fair a bunch of the Irish people from the Mountain and a bunch from Renfrew got into it. And when it was all over, there was one of them from the Mountain who was quite dead. So they had an inquest and a hearing that dragged on for weeks and weeks and wasn't getting anywhere because nobody knew anything or everybody said they knew nothing. Finally the frustrated magistrate issued his decree.

" 'The hearing is completed,' he said. 'I have decided that anybody with a skull that thin shouldn't have been at the Renfrew Fair.' "

*

Around and About

Storyland

Driving north out of Renfrew on Highway No. 417, you come to the Storyland turnoff. Follow the signs to the Storyland site perched on a high plateau overlooking the Ottawa River. Just before Storyland proper you come to MacKenzie's Hill, which has a lookout to afford you one of the great Valley sweeps across the Ottawa River to the Quebec side.

Storyland is a moppets' paradise, providing the youngsters with 280 familiar full-size carved storybook characters from fairy tales on a 40-acre wooded site. There is a wildlife museum, a picnic area, a two-acre playground, an 18-hole mini-golf course as well as paddle boats and pony rides. Adults will want to climb up and see the Ottawa Valley from Champlain's Lookout.

Douglas

You can get to Douglas by many scenic back-country roads. One way is by Highway No. 60 direct, or you can go out Renfrew "the back way" on No. 132, turning onto No. 513 at Dacre, and thence into Douglas. *The Union Star Cheese Factory* is a landmark on No. 513, so you might prefer that way if you and your family want to see cheese made and buy some of the delicious produce from this 90-year-old farmers' cooperative — one of the few in the country that has not succumbed to Kraft or some such all-engulfing corporation.

Situated at the Third Chute on the Bonnechere River, some 12 miles west of Renfrew, the site of Douglas today was well known to the early lumbermen who had to get their timber past the 21-foot fall of water. In the 1820s, as lumbering activities extended up the river, a few settlers followed the lumbermen's trails, moving in to establish farms that would supply the lumber camps. Judge John G. Malloch of Perth, moving far afield in his entrepreneurial quests, bought land in the Third Chute area, surveyed it for a village in 1853, and named it Douglas after Douglas in Lanarkshire, Scotland. Thomas Bell built a stone grist mill there in the 1840s, operational until just a few years ago. Charles Merrick's mill upstream at the Fourth Chute also was built in the 1840s. In 1853 Alexander Murray of the Geological Survey of Canada remarked upon the "remarkable subterranean channel" at the site.

St. Patrick's Day in Douglas

It is ironic that Douglas, pioneered by the Scots, has become a major centre for St. Patrick's Day celebrations. For many years now, hundreds of Valley people have gathered in the town's hotel for very lively, but generally not obstreperous, celebrations in honour of Ireland's patron saint. Doorways are decorated in green, green lawn lights appear in front of some houses, and there is a grand general "wearing of the green," with the familiar singing, dancing, fiddling — and drinking. Valley songmaker, the late Mac Beattie, eulogized the Douglas St. Patrick Day celebrations in this lyric:

"Sure there's fun there — everyone's there
From the banks of the Bonnechere
From the point right up to Killaloe
All the O'Gormans and the O'Reillys
All the Manions and the Kileys,
All the Irish are having a do."

MILL HOUSE, BONNECHERE CAVES

The Bonnechere Caves have been opened to the public at the site of John Knight's grist mill at the Fourth Chute. The mill house and mill ruins are part of this tourist attraction.

For many years Douglas was the home town of Valley writer and storyteller Vi Dooling, now retired to Renfrew. This story of Vi's is great because it is indigenous to the area and, of course, true:

Now in Douglas in the early days there was a wonderful man named Canon Quartermain. He looked after the Children's Aid and neglected children and poor widows and misguided and pregnant girls and all that sort of thing. So when the Good Roads Gang put roads through Douglas in 1922, he got word that one of the Douglas girls was expecting a baby and she was not married. So Canon Quartermain went to visit her.

" 'Tell me, my child, who is the father of this baby that you will be having soon?'

" 'I can't say, Reverend,' she replied.

" 'I am going to see that he does right by you and marries you.'

" 'I really can't say,' the girl answered.

" 'You must know at least his name,' the Canon said testily. 'I have to have a name to put down here if I am going to help you.'

" 'Well, Canon, well — to be honest with you now,' faltered the girl from Douglas, 'I guess you will just have to put down "The Good Roads Gang." ' "

✳

The Bonnechere Caves

In Douglas turn west at the bank on the main street and follow the signs to the Fourth Chute Road, where under a hill of limestone 500 million years old lie the wonderful caves.

A Bonnechere native of the walled city of Chester in England (and thereby a lover of stone), spelunker Tom Woodward made his way to Pembroke, Ontario, where he heard rumours going back to 1853 of caves under the Bonnechere. Armed only with his courage, an inflatable raft, and a flashlight, Woodward was exploring the caves by 1953. After several narrow escapes he had a portion of the caves drained of water, lighted, and open to the public by 1955. Since then, more tunnels and passages have been opened. Today, the sightseer is treated to twisting passages winding through rock cut into tiers, stalactites — rock icicles — and the wonders achieved by the unremitting action of water on stone. Tom Woodward can answer questions, tell stories, and point out the fossils of coral and sea creatures entombed in the caves. Geology students from both American and Canadian universities come here to study.

The caves have been opened at the site of John Knight's first grist mill, *circa* 1840. The picturesque ruins are only part of the scenic pleasures of the Fourth Chute. The Bonnechere at this point is clear, swift, and lovely. Picnic tables and toilet facilities are available, but swimming is not allowed. There is a Rotary Club supervised beach five miles away at Eganville.

Eganville

Out of Douglas you can follow Highway No. 60 into Eganville, the town of the Fifth Chute of the Bonnechere, founded by lumbermen and settled by Irish, both Catholic and Protestant. Throughout its history, the Catholics lived on the south side of the bridge over the Bonnechere and the Protestants clung to the hills on the north side.

As might be expected, this is another one of John Egan's towns, although James Wadsworth preceded Egan chronologically when he came from Ireland in 1826 and began clearing a portion of land later known as "The Farm." During the period 1826–37 Wadsworth went into lumbering on his own, employing several men. It was during this time the earliest settlers came: John Egan, Robert Mills, John Coyne, William Jessup, Robert Turner, Robert Foy, and Abraham Roland. Egan purchased The Farm from Wadsworth in 1837 and began his enterprises at the Fifth Chute, building slides to facilitate the movement of his timber, operating a sawmill to cut his lumber, and opening a store to supply the growing community. Provisions for this store were brought by canoe and boat all the way up the Ottawa River from Bytown to Renfrew at the mouth of the Bonnechere and then up to Eganville.

Nestled in the centre of a series of lakes and hills and surrounding scenic hills, Eganville has become over the years a summertime tourist and cottage town. Its off-the-beaten-track peace and its tranquility have attracted a number of young people seeking alternative lifestyles. One of the results of this influx of newcomers has been the opening of many craft outlets and artists' studios.

The Granary, a restored historical site on Eganville's main street, is one of the few special places to eat in the Upper Ottawa Valley. *The Treasure Chest* at 227 Bridge Street specializes in hand-made-to-measure garments, local craft items, yarns from various companies, craft supplies, woodwork, quilts, afghans, and baby items. *Country Sunshine*, in a restored building on a century farm outside of Eganville, features locally made country crafts, kids' stuff, folk art, collectibles, and antiques. It is five miles west of Eganville on Highway No. 512 to the Donegal Road; signs are posted along the way. *Homestead Galleries*, also a little way out of town, sells antiques, collectibles, and accessories and has a furniture-restoration service specializing in wicker and caning, lathe work, brass and copper polishing, and custom wood repairs. It is located on Sand Road off No. 512, two miles from Strickland's Store.

DIRECTIONS

From Eganville, you can return to Ottawa via Highway No. 5, which you pick up at Kelly's Corner, into Renfrew, then onto No. 17 for a direct route home. Or you can take the tour along the Opeongo Line, described in the next chapter.

Chapter 7

ALONG
the
OPEONGO LINE

Preamble

The Opeongo Line is an 1840s settlement road running from Farrell's Landing on the Ottawa River near Castleford westward through Renfrew, Dacre, Esmonde, Clontarf, Brudenell, Vanbrugh, Wilno, Barry's Bay, and into Bark Lake, where it ends. Originally, when the Line was conceived as a line of defense against the Americans, it was intended that it run all the way to Opeongo Lake in Algonquin Park. But long before that, it began to dawn on even the unsuspecting settlers that the Laurentian Shield was no place to farm and that the timber at the rate it was being depleted was going to run out.

To complete an exploration of the 70-mile-long Opeongo Line is to make an astonishing leap back into the nineteenth century, into a past held almost intact where you may still view the square-timber log buildings hewn and erected from the virgin timbers by the first settlers to set foot on the soil of the new land. Today, some of the farms are still owned, lived in, and even worked by descendants of those pioneers. Where else in the world can you

1 CASTLEFORD (FARRELL'S LANDING)
2 DACRE
3 ESMOND
4 CLONTARF
5 BRUDENELL
6 VANBURGH
7 WILNO
8 FERGUSLEA
9 HOPEFIELD

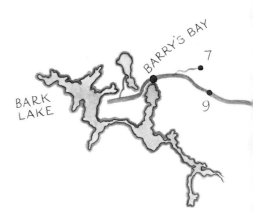

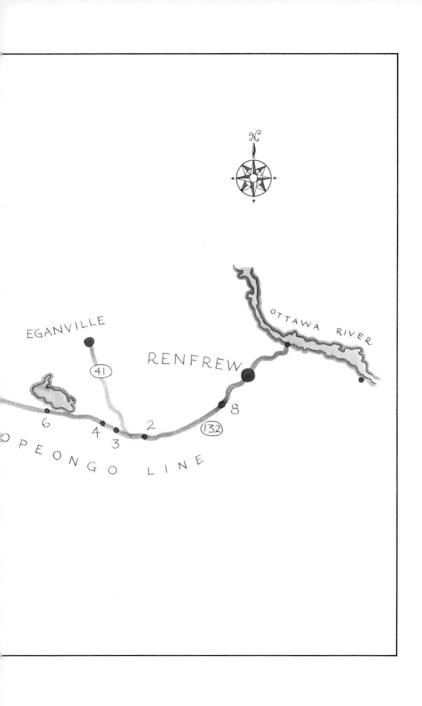

travel back into your own beginnings like that?

A trip up the Opeongo Line takes you through some of the most beautiful — if unproductive — landscape in Ontario, climbing through the haunted Opeongo Hills, winding past clear lakes and deserted homesteads, weaving through the thronging ghosts of those post-and-chain men fighting their way through the dense forest, the mosquitoes, and the black flies to survey the Line; of excited timber barons hiking up the Line with their tallymen to calculate the riches of a timber stand; of teams of horses and shantymen in caravans streaming up the Line to fell the monoliths of the forest.

PREPARATIONS

Except in towns like Renfrew, Dacre, and Barry's Bay, there are very few restaurants and gas stations. I recommend that you pack picnic lunches and fill up with gas.

You will want to get out and walk a little or perhaps even hike a piece along some of the side roads — and certainly a good part of Newfoundout is not accessible except on foot — so wear your hiking clothes and boots.

It will not be possible to explore all the deviations in one day, so you should choose those that look especially appealing to you. You can save the unexplored ones for another visit to the Opeongo Line. Have your camera loaded for those sights you will want to capture on film.

HISTORY

The Opeongo Line is richly peopled with the ghosts of early pioneers, river giants, shantymen, timber barons, remittance men. As it leaves the Ottawa and heads northwest toward Renfrew, the road keeps a fairly steady course. Then, outside of Renfrew, it takes a sidewinder through Ferguslea, makes it back on a fairly steady southwesterly course again on Highway No. 132, with just the occasional jog as it heads toward the crossroads of Dacre.

Outside of Dacre, the road takes a sharp right, which makes the traveller think he might be going to Douglas, Eganville, or Killaloe. But within a few hundred feet the Opeongo veers to the left, into the Opeongo Hills, jogging its footloose and fancy-free way through Clontarf, Esmonde, Brudenell, finally stumbling into Barry's Bay. From this town, the road steers toward Opeongo Lake. But it never makes it, dying along the way at Bark Lake.

According to Ottawa Valley legend, the reason the Opeongo joggles, veers, and stumbles is because the original line was blazed by one Dan MacCauley, whose fondness for local grog is still touted 160 years later — in a country of hard drinkers surely a reputation *sans pareil*. In 1851 when post-and-chain man Hamlet Burritt of Burritt's Rapids was pushing his way through cold, heat, black flies, mosquitoes, over mountains, through swamps, and across lakes, Dan MacCauley was one of Burritt's survey crew. And in his diaries Burritt reports on his problems with the incorrigible Dan. An entry from May 19, 1851, reads: "Sent him [Dan] out to meet Mr. Bell and to buy him a hat but I think he spent it for grog."

❡ STORY

I can tell you a funny story about the blazing of the Opeongo Line. Everyone will tell you that it was so crooked because it was blazed by drunken Dan MacCauley. But that's not true at all. There was this blind Indian from Golden Lake and he had an uncanny knack for finding roads through the bush. He worked for the Carswell Lumber Company of Renfrew. And he blazed the Madawaska Hill for the Chief MacNab. Yes, sir. It was no drunken Dan MacCauley but a blind Indian from the Golden Lake Reserve that blazed out the Opeongo Trail."

✽

But Dan MacCauley had not blazed the original Opeongo Line as a means of travelling from groggery to groggery. Like so many early roads in Canada, the Opeongo was conceived to meet military needs. Following the armed skirmishes of the War of 1812, there was government concern for alternate supply routes in the event of a more serious struggle with the Americans. An east-west route was considered strategic and, as early as 1821, surveyor-general Thomas Ridout at York wrote of the necessity to explore a line or road from the Ottawa, or Grand River as it was called then, into the hinterlands of the Upper Valley.

Sir Francis Bond Head, Lieutenant Governor of Upper Canada (and, incidentally, influential friend and drinking pal of that other great imbiber, the Last Laird MacNab of White Lake and Arnprior), directed action to be taken. Various army officers, surveyors, explorers, and adventurers began to examine the lands. Among these men, coming by canoe, was Alexander Sherriff, son of Charles Sherriff of Quebec City, who travelled through the Upper Ottawa Valley in 1829, bringing back glowing reports of the luxuriant hardwood forests, which he mistakenly offered as clear evidence of good farming land, "millions of acres of it," as he described it in reports.

Following close on Sherriff's heels, Lieutenant F.H. Baddeley in 1836 was much less optimistic, describing the soil everywhere throughout the Ottawa country as "light, sandy and very often very shallow."

Nevertheless, a few years later, a definite proposal went forth "to build a winter road from the present head of Steamboat Navigation on the Ottawa River at Farrell's Point to the mouth of the Magnetawan or the French River on the Georgian Bay of Lake Huron, adopting a road-line drawn by Mr. Bell through the townships of Horton, Adamston, Brougham, and Grattan, and thence in a westerly direction to the Great Opeongo Lake in the headwaters of a branch of the Madawaska River." In the meantime, the slender footpath or blazed trail through the woods was being established by a motley collection of hikers, squatters, settlers, shantymen, itinerant preachers and teachers, surveyors, tinkers, millers, blacksmiths, soldiers of the King, fiddlers, tale-bearers, and timber barons.

In 1855, government land agent T.P. French set up shop in Mount St. Patrick and wrote his pamphlet entitled *Information for Intending Settlers on the Ottawa and Opeongo Road and its Vicinity*, dated Canada West, February 1857. The pamphlet was meant as an inducement to the starving Irish in the midst of recovering from their potato famine, and to the heartbroken Scots who were being cleared off their lands so that English absentee landowners could graze sheep. If Mr. French did not lie in his PR releases, he might be said to have stretched the truth, especially when he promised "good soil" and "snow that did not fall in sufficient quantities to obstruct roads or make travel difficult."

The years 1850–90 were the peak settlement and productive years along the Opeongo. By the turn of the century the lumber barons had scalped the landscape. The timbering business had peaked and begun to decline. The last drive went down the Ottawa in 1911. Wood cutting could no longer sustain the marginal farms along the beautiful Opeongo. Hard economic facts froze the Opeongo country just as time can petrify wood. For the majority of those who stayed on their holdings on the Opeongo, there was no way to "move up" to frame and brick. The log buildings stood.

And the young people left. Clan ties, blood ties, love of beauty, fiddlin' good times, bonds forged in adversity, guilt feelings about the farm, a gut attachment to the Valley — its song, its dance, its accent, its humour, its lore, its people — none of these things could hold the young ones any longer on the depleted land.

"They are going, going, going and we cannot bid them stay."

Down the Opeongo they went in almost tribal procession, to the West, to the States, to the big cities, to the mines of Cobalt, Kirkland Lake, Haileybury.

DIRECTIONS

Take any route you choose to Castleford on the Ottawa River below Renfrew. You can go directly up Highway No. 17 to the turnoff at Renfrew marked "Business Section." Or you can explore the back roads through Carp, South March, Galetta, and Arnprior, where, if you go out the "back way" along Madawaska Boulevard, you will hit one of my favourite byways, the River Road, Highway No. 3, which takes you directly to Castleford. If you want to spend a full day on the Opeongo Line, soaking yourself in the nineteenth century, experiencing your heritage and your beginnings, then I recommend that you travel directly and quickly up No. 17 to the turnoff toward Castleford, County Road No. 20.

Your tour will be enhanced by being brave enough to turn off the Opeongo down any side road that beckons you. I promise that you will discover log heritage treasures that will impress and delight you. I urge you to be adventuresome and deviate away from the Opeongo Line proper for another reason. Since I first began travelling it 25 years ago and since my children first began entertaining themselves by counting the log buildings along the route, many of the heritage treasures have been torn down and trucked away. So it is still down the narrow, hilly, often overgrown side roads — especially in the Wilno–Barry's Bay area — that you will discover the original, untouched, unmutilated buildings. Be as creative as you please about the explorations you make.

When historian Marilyn Miller did her detailed study of the buildings on the Opeongo, she used miles and mileposts as the road measurement. I have had to follow this. Set your odometer, if you have one, at Castleford, and if necessary translate the miles into kilometres (roughly double).

Braeside and *Sand Point*

Out of Arnprior on the River Road, Highway No. 3, before you come to Castleford and the beginning of the Opeongo Line, you will pass through two charming early riverside towns clinging to small, low hills along the Ottawa on the Ontario side and looking over the river to the mountains of Quebec. Both these villages are mixes of their early history and the relayering of some superior modern housing. Braeside is the site of a number of Gillies lumber company workmen's houses, a small Gillies office remaining on the original mill site, and two outstanding Gillies summer "cottages," both on the west side of the main street, one brown frame (now converted to apartments) with exceptionally high-peaked gables and the larger second one with great screened porches and stone pillars at the entrance, now a bed and breakfast.

Sand Point was the site of early timber baron Alexander Macdonnell's empire. Surrounded by rare acacia trees and a wrought-iron fence with stone pillars, MacDonnell's stone house remaines here, well preserved, just above the former departure point of the old Sand Point-to-Norway Bay ferry. Macdonnell's white frame Roman Catholic church is also roadside here.

Castleford and *Farrell's Landing*

Castleford owes its name to young Lieutenant Christopher James Bell, who was born in 1795, in Castleford, Yorkshire, England, and lost a leg in a naval battle on Lake Champlain during the War of 1812. In 1817 the enterprising Bell immigrated to the military settlement of Perth, where because of his rank he was entitled to a

GILLIES SUMMER COTTAGE, BRAESIDE

Now a bed and breakfast, this "cottage" was once the summer home of the Gillies family. Braeside is the site of other Gillies' establishments, including a small office on the original mill grounds.

land grant of 800 acres. He took up more land near Pakenham and Carleton Place but finally exchanged his holdings there for some of Owen Quinn's grants at the junction of the Bonnechere and Ottawa rivers. By 1829 he had built a sawmill and a grist mill at the First Chute, a 30-foot-high falls about a mile from the mouth of the Bonnechere. The site became known as Castleford. When Bell died in 1836, his industry passed into other hands and the settlement emphasis shifted to the shores of Chats Lake at Arnprior. On the River Road a plaque commemorates Bell's early enterprises, and the bridge across the Bonnechere on the scenic River Road between Arnprior and Castleford (part of the original road from Bytown to Pembroke, opened in 1852) has been named after Bell.

A little farther up the River Road from Castleford proper you will come to an aluminum-clad schoolhouse — now a grocery store — overlooking the Ottawa, and a motely collection of cottages and campsites, one of which is called Grandview Cottages. There are a few scattered log buildings here nearby the Red Barn century stone house and farmstead with commercial riding stables. This is where the Opeongo Line settlers, for the most part, landed — at Farrell's Landing on Farrell's Point. If you are really keen you can get out of your car and on the Grandview Cottage property find the original old grassy trail they walked up after disembarking from the boats or canoes that had brought them upriver from Scotland, England, France, Germany, Poland, and Ireland.

At Farrell's Landing there was long ago "The Woodyard" — acres of sawn wood lying in storage to be used in the early woodburning boats on the river.

❡ S T O R Y

Edward Farrell was born in County Sligo, Ireland, about 1810 and by the 1830s had established a stopping-place on the Ottawa River, Lot 10, 9th Concession, of Horton Township, a site eventually called Farrell's Landing. Edward Prince of Wales visited Farrell's Landing on his 1860 trip up the Ottawa. Most accounts of this trip lead one to think his farthest stop upriver was the entertainment provided for him at Dan McLachlin's house in Arnprior, or at Alexander Macdonnell's riverside empire at Sand Point. But the Castleford tale is that the

178

steamer proceeded to Farrell's Landing, where a piece of red material was duly spread out to serve as a carpet for the royal feet when the Prince disembarked. It was evidently a happy and informal welcome, and the Prince, feeling at home, tossed young Josh Farrell, then aged seven, up in his arms and made him laugh. When the royal party departed downriver — they went no farther so far as we know now — the red cloth was left behind to be rescued by a Farrell and made into a skirt for one of young Joshua's sisters.

Renfrew

At Highway No. 3 and County Road No. 20, there is a schoolhouse-cum-grocery store. Turn west and drive along No. 20, where you will see many original log farm homesteads. When you come to Highway No. 17 you will note on the south side one of the very few stone houses along the Opeongo. Go straight across No. 17 into Renfrew's business section. The Opeongo wound through Renfrew village in the pioneer days. For settlers coming in on the Opeongo the 1840s Hudson Bay Factor John Lorne McDougall had already opened his store. After 1865 newcomers could cross the Bonnechere in Renfrew over Kearney's swinging bridge. You still can today.

Renfrew formally became a village in 1858. We assume that by then it had stopping-places to accommodate the incoming Opeongo Line settlers. Certainly the Orange-Wright Hotel, on the corner of Arthur and Albert streets, appears in Wallings Map of 1863. McDougall's stone grist mill began in 1855, and about the same time Samuel Francis's axe factory and William MacKay's sawmill.

By midcentury Renfrew had blacksmith shops, a carriage shop, a tannery, a cooper's shop, carpenter shops, a log schoolhouse, a brewery, a post office, a shoemaker, doctors, harness makers, general stores, and churches. One of these early blacksmith shops still stands today on the corner of Arthur and Raglan streets.

Continue on Raglan Street until you come to stoplights and the M.J. O'Brien buildings (with the movie house downstairs). Turn left, go past the Renfrew *Mercury* along Opeongo Road until you come to an outstanding high-gabled Victorian brick with a number of barns unused but still standing, all set back in tall trees. This is the Carswell Estate.

Of all the nouveau-riche class — the timber kings of the Valley — Bob Carswell was the only one who built his baronial castle on the Opeongo. It remains there today, only slightly altered, on the outskirts of Renfrew. Some time ago his granddaughter, Joan MacKay, overlooking the carved drive of the Carswell Estate, gave a colourful reminiscence of lumbering days along the Opeongo.

❡ S T O R Y

This story came from the late Joan Mackay, descendant of the Carswell lumbering family of Renfrew:

Every November they would start from here for the shanties. The horses, the sleigh loaded with supplies, the teamsters, the men would be lined up here as far as you could see waiting for Grandpa. And then he would come out on the veranda, all bundled up in his huge beaver hat and coat, and he would shout 'Hoy!' And that procession would start off down the Opeongo to the lumber camps."

*

Ferguslea

Continue on the road past the Carswell Estate. Until a few years ago, the old original corduroy road ran in front of Carswell's. On this jog you will pass several working farms with many log outbuildings. And on the north, clearly visible on a hillside site, stands one completely deserted farm homestead with a score of outbuildings, including a windowless honey house. Once a showplace along the Opeongo, it still belongs to original settlers. Farther on you pass a couple of original log homesteads, still working farms.

The road winds back onto Highway No. 132, again passing a number of original log homesteads, until it comes to another sidewinder into Ferguslea, demarcated by a sign pointing south, "Opeongo Road." Ferguslea is the hamlet founded in 1840 by Ferguson when he fled the Last Laird MacNab's tyranny at White Lake and Waba and, with a group of his clansmen, came up from Renfrew. Ferguslea was the site of the next stopping-place, Culhane's, once a massive Victorian frame, now cut down to an anonymous bungalow.

The Quilty Farm

The next three-mile section of the Opeongo Line from mile 14 to mile 17 has more farmsteads with log buildings that approximate the nineteenth-century landscape, particularly the deserted Reid farm. To the south you will pass signposts marking the Whelan Road, settled by numbers of Whelans and a lovely road for meandering. You will also pass the first of three signposts south to Mount St. Patrick — all roads led to Mount St. Patrick, indeed — and at mile 17 on the north side you will come to a signpost marking Adamston Country Road No. 10.

Just past this turnoff on the south side you will come to the Quilty Farm, one of the century farms on the Opeongo Line still worked by descendants of the first pioneers. The green and white frame house surrounded by log outbuildings is set down a long lane through fields demarcated by stone fences from the load "stoned" by Leonard Quilty's ancestors. His wife's family, the Louths from near the Ulster border, during the potato famine of the 1840s walked up from Castleford to new land along the Opeongo.

From the time they arrived on the Opeongo Line, the Quiltys were not only industrious farmers but people who gave leadership to and became involved in the community. Michael Quilty, Leonard's father, introduced the telephone to the Opeongo Line, the Quilty family maintaining the 22 miles of lines and repairing its 16 phones until taken over by Bell Telephone in 1945. Imagine a party line with only 16 users! Michael Quilty helped to organize the country road system and became a councillor, reeve, and school board member for years for Adamston Township.

¶ STORY

Leonard Quilty told me this story:

My father, Michael Quilty, before he was married around 1900, worked as a shantyman cutting square timber in the bush up the Line. The family still has here his broadaxe. Later when he quit the bush and returned to farming, he walked from farm to farm along the Opeongo to set up the first rural mail delivery service. In order to qualify for mail service, my father had to get a certain number of people to sign on for mailboxes. He ended up short by two. But that didn't stop him. He bought two extra boxes for a couple of old lads around here — and the mail came through."

*

Shamrock

At mile 18, just past the junction of the Opeongo and Adamston County Road No. 11, you arrive at the remains of Shamrock village, comprised now of a few houses and a number of log buildings. To me it was always distinguished by one of the two log stores I know of along the Opeongo, the other being Pat Lynch's store off the Line at McDougall and still functioning. But the Shamrock log store ceased business a number of years ago, and, as far as I can tell now, is at present a residence.

Just past Shamrock you become aware of the beginning of your climb into the mountains. At mile 19 you pass Curly Jack Keilly's log barn ruins with a tree growing up out of the centre of it, now an Opeongo landmark.

You come shortly to the second turnoff south to Mount St. Patrick, another good road for meandering off onto, down past Johnny Kielly's log house, toward the Sammon settlement and the Kielly settlement. Also at this junction, a little to the west, is the abandoned Enright homestead, almost hidden now in overgrowth and trees.

❡ STORY

The late Johnny Kiely played the mouth organ as he told me this story:

When I was young we went to dances and dances and never a drop of whisky and we'd dance until the morning. You danced in the Sammon Settlement with four or five violin players and all kinds of girls in every house and no whisky — lots of girls and lots of music — two Lynches, two Godda lads, two Murphy lads, and the Murphy girl could play the violin — you go to Kinnelley's, you go to Christie Murphy's, you go to Godda, you go to Hawley's, you go to Sammon's."

Dacre

Outside of Renfrew and Barry's Bay, Dacre (on Highway No. 132) was the largest settlement on the Opeongo, and what remains of it constitutes the best example of a nineteenth-century Colonization Road village. Once so thriving that it was divided into Upper and Lower Dacre, it is located at the crossroads of the Opeongo Colonization Road and the old road leading from the Bonnechere to the Madawaska River, a route so important to the shantymen and timber barons. This road connects Eganville, Balaclava, Mount St. Patrick, and Calabogie to Dacre. Dacre from its original Lower to Upper Dacre stretches from mile 23 to 24.

Dacre was an important service centre for early settlers and a popular stopping-place for shantymen. It has been told that there was once a stopping-place on each of Dacre's four corners. However, evidence so far has supported the existence of only two: the huge log Ryan-Godda stopping-place on the northeast corner, dismantled and moved to Deep River, and the Legris stopping-place, demolished some years ago.

¶ STORY

This story was told to me on the Opeongo Line:

Do you mind the time that Michael Godda came home from the bush in a box? He was foreman for Booth on the Bonnechere and he ordered his men into a log jam and they refused to go and he said, 'All right, you sons of bitches, I'll do it myself.' And he did. And they brought him home to Dacre in a box. The Godda women — good lookers they were, too — couldn't run a hotel without a man and they sold to the Ryans, and the Ryans died off and went away, and it sat empty for a long time, the biggest log lumberman's hotel in the whole Valley, and then they came and moved it to Deep River. Shame. Should have stayed where it belonged, where it grew up, I say."

*

Although much of the village has been destroyed or left to fall into ruin, there are enough valuable buildings left to make the site worth preserving as an example of a Colonization Road village: clapboard village houses, the imposing Victorian frame — a

183

Legris house — an old general store with living quarters combined, the Dacre schoolhouse on the Madawaska–Bonnechere road running through the village, and close by the lovely little white frame Baptist church. The church has a date of 1866 painted on it, and it is probably made of square timbers later covered with shiplap.

The Dacre area abounds in legend, particularly the story of Rory Macdonald, who had his eyes "gouged out in a fight at Dacre," some say with an older man (*in extremis*) who was driven to use such a method of fighting off his adversary. Others say that Rory Macdonald "always looked for it." At any rate, Rory solved his disability problem by playing his fiddle in the lumber camps for money. His little house sits at Dacre yet, on the north side of the village right on the Opeongo below road level, an insul-brick red-coloured house, probably log underneath.

✱

Dacre might well provide a good family stopping-place. There is a Canada Goose Preservation Centre on Constant Creek in the village. There's also a picnic park on the Opeongo, just as you turn off Highway No. 41 out of Dacre, which might better suit your needs. And you can visit the Magnetic Hill as well.

Magnetic Hill

Yes, Ontario does have a Magnetic Hill, although much less publicized than the one in the Atlantic Provinces! Continue along Highway No. 132, past the junction with No. 41 for about a mile. There you will find clearly marked signs to the Magnetic Hill.

Dacre also provides the third turnoff south to Mount St. Patrick, travelling past Candiac Ski Hills and on to one of the treasures of the Opeongo area, Kinnelly's Mountain.

Opeongo Road

Go back to the junction of Highway Nos. 132 and 41 and turn north on No. 41 as though you were headed for Eganville. But only a few paces from the corners you will come to a sign pointing west saying "Opeongo Road." Turn here. This section of the Opeongo is one of the best representations of a late nineteenth-century farming-lumbering landscape, with its numerous log-constructed farmsteads. Up until a few years ago the road was still gravel and narrow. Some of the loveliest scenery in the Colonization Road area appears in this section of the road, stretching from No. 41 to Barry's Bay and climbing through the Opeongo Hills.

The Opeongo Oasis

Just past the Opeongo Line Picnic Park, on the north side of the road you will come to a somewhat faded handmade sign saying "Opeongo Oasis." It marks the site of a renowned clear mountain runoff spring at which Opeongo travellers have stopped to drink for 150 years. Patriarch of the Opeongo Line Allan Davidson had the sign put up and keeps the site cleared.

But there is more than just pure clear water here. The legend of the Opeongo Oasis is that the ground in summertime and the snow in wintertime surrounding the oasis was always "covered with blood." In the early days Dacre's four hotels, hours unlimited, sold the potent high wines. Settlers, squatters, farmers, shantymen used to buy their high wines at Ryan's or the Legris stopping-place in Dacre and continue on up the road to the Opeongo spring to stop and dilute their liquor with the clear spring water. Here the men would stop and blather, and have a drink or two for the road, and fall to arguing and then into fisticuffs — so much so that "the snow was always covered with blood."

Esmonde

One might weep for Esmonde, for all that is really left of it is St. Joseph's Roman Catholic Church, a community centre, a house, and a few draggled remains of what was the substantial landmark, the Curry homestead and post office. When I first saw the Curry place some 15 years ago, I could not count the number of log buildings surrounding it. The house, one of the most beautiful on the Opeongo, was still filled with its nineteenth-century furnishings — and all had been left as though someone had died overnight and no one had ever returned. I wrote to the owners to ask what we might do to preserve the historical site. I received no answer.

However, there are a few good homesteads left along this stretch as well as S.S. No. 5, a bleached pink frame schoolhouse with a perennial fridge on its porch. This is the schoolhouse to which the children of Newfoundout walked eight miles down the mountains to obtain their three Rs.

The Allan Davidson Farm

The Allan Davidson farm, at mile 26 of the Opeongo Line, is situated in a hollow before the land climbs the Opeongo Mountains to overlook Lake Clear. At this juncture the crossroad north goes to Eganville, the major shopping centre, and south to the now-abandoned farming settlement of Newfoundout.

Allan Davidson considers his complex of log buildings the finest in the country, and he says it with great pride. "My people came in before the blaze," he will tell you, "on a lumbering road in from the Bonnechere River. I remember my great-grandmother telling me about soldiers marching through the bush during the War of 1812."

The Davidsons came to this large tract of land before the Opeongo Line was opened to settlers, and the log buildings of which Davidson is so carefully preservative go back to the earlier times — the shanty-style sheds, for instance — while the house, probably a "third house," was built in the twentieth century, *circa* 1930. The pride of Davidson's heritage collection is hidden in bush behind his present house; it is the square-timber "first" Davidson house in which, according to family tradition, William Bell stayed when he was surveying the Line. "Surveyor Robert Bell stayed there with my people when he was working on the Line; nowhere else to stay. And I wouldn't let anyone touch it for love or money. No one should be allowed to take a single log building off the road," snarls 80-year-old Allan Davidson of Davidson's Corners on the Opeongo Line.

Four generations ago in the 1820s, Davidson's ancestors were among the first settlers to trek up the Opeongo, then only a cross between a deer run and an Indian trail. They squatted on the land. But if they had no mortgage payments to face, they were confronted by a far more formidable hurdle: that of wresting their land from the Laurentian Shield.

Today, Davidson owns 1,000 acres on the Opeongo Line, most of it still in bush. He cuts wood, fixes machines, drives a tractor and a truck, keeps his own private museum, and, every fall, along with the rest of the male population of the Upper Ottawa, goes deer hunting. Thorughout the remainder of the year, as he puts it, "I kill every bear I see."

Last year, Old Man Davidson drove his tractor up the mountain to help a man who had car trouble. When the tractor brakes slipped and the machine took off down the mountainside, he held on for dear life. Instead of being found dead at the foot of the mountain, he was found with just a "few almighty bruises." "And it didn't keep me from deer-hunting this fall either," he boasts. Davidson hunts 700 miles north, above Kapuskasing, Ontario.

Besides being a forthright, almost invincible, tough old Irishman, Davidson is also a simple man with little formal education. He went only as far as Book IV (Grade 8) at the little red schoolhouse, the S.S. No. 5, Grattan, down the Opeongo, a few miles from the homestead.

Raycroft Century Farm and *Clontarf*

At mile 27, just before St. Clement's Anglican Church and little graveyard, the Raycrofts, one of the first families to settle in the area, according to Allan Davidson, kept a stopping-place here for generations back. The century farmhouse, set on a hill with a wide sweep of the road preceding it, is very visible and must have been a welcome sight indeed to the weary wayfarers walking or travelling with horse and vehicle along the Opeongo in the nineteenth century.

St. Clement's Church probably dates back to mid-nineteenth century and is most likely square timber underneath its siding. A small cemetery east of the church has German inscriptions on some of the tombstones, indicating the German settlement of this area. The church is in good condition and the grounds are well kept.

Beyond St. Clement's Church and Raycroft's hilltop stoppingplace, from mile 27 to mile 29, the road settlement of Clontarf today encompasses some of the finest working farms along the Opeongo.

On the south side stands a white frame farmhouse (log underneath), now owned by Valiquettes, with hillside-tiered barns to the east. The Edwards log homestead, set way down southside in the valley with the Opeongo Hills behind it, has amongst its collection of ancient log buildings the original shanty, scoop-roofed, in which 11 children were born. The O'Brien homestead on the south has a collection of very old frame buildings as well as log.

On the north, Mrs. Herman Gierman's collection of heritage log buildings is hidden, one of them with an intact dinner bell and another with a scooped roof. The Mutoys on the north have a line of great long barns marching against the skyline. Also on the north stands the Rose flat-top house, its land climbing, climbing behind it, almost to the sky.

Lutheran Church

At mile 33 you may want to pause for this steepled and most picturesquely set little Lutheran church, with asbestos siding exterior but probably log underneath, dating back to 1850. There is a small cemetery to the side. Until very recently the church was opened once a year for Thanksgiving services. A good place to stretch your legs in peace and tranquility.

Plaunt's Stopping-Place

Atop the next big hill sits Xavier Plaunt's big white square frame stopping-place, very well preserved, with board barns to the west of it.

¶ S T O R Y

This is another story told to me on my Opeongo Line travels:

In the 1840s a canny newcomer by the name of Xavier Plaunt set out from Renfrew, went a day's journey by foot, stopped, and built Plaunt's Hotel on top of what was later named for him as Plaunt's Mountain. It was not until 1858 that the Opeongo Road was declared "fit" for wagon traffic. Plaunt knew that his clientele would have to come by foot through rain and heat, mud and hills, carrying their few possessions and their small children on their backs. And at the end of that long, long day's

LUTHERAN CHURCH, OPEONGO LINE

*This church dates back to 1850 when it was constructed from log.
At one time abandoned, the church was until recently opened
only for Thanksgiving services.*

walk into the wilderness there would be "thanks to God for Plaunt's Hotel!" It was said for many years to be the best in Opeongo country. As the traffic on the road increased and the wagons and sleighs carrying men and supplies to the lumber camps reached almost procession-like numbers, Plaunt is said to have collected his revenues in silver in a five-gallon pail kept for that purpose only.

✻

Kosmack Century Farm

At the top of the next hill, still climbing above sea level, Kosmack's century farm gives a spectacular view of the Ottawa Valley and Round Lake. This is another great working farm on the Opeongo Line and is made up of buildings from the earliest settlement years down to the modern roadside bungalow, which is probably in use for one of the younger generations of Kosmacks on the land.

❡ S T O R Y

The late Tom Murray of Barry's Bay told this one:

My mother told me about how the shantymen used to walk up the Opeongo Line. She told me about a big man named McGillivray. He weighed over 300 pounds and he was walking by her door and asked for some water. My mother brought him a dipperful. But he said to her, 'Good God, my girl! That's no good to me! Bring me the pail!' "

✻

Vanbrugh Schoolhouse

Vanbrugh Schoolhouse, at mile 37 of the Opeongo, dates back to mid-nineteenth century. The name of this section of settlement along the old Colonization Road, again indicates settlers of German origin. The square-timber schoolhouse is in good condition

190

and is currently in use as a house. It is the only log schoolhouse I know of along the Opeongo, but it is quite likely that some of the remaining schoolhouses, although overlaid with frame and shiplap today, were originally log underneath.

Brudenell

At the junction of the Peterson Junction Colonization Road to the south and another road to Eganville to the north lies Brudenell. This is an excellent place to explore on foot. Like Dacre, Brudenell was once a thriving, lusty, vital crossroads village on the Opeongo, with hotels, stores, houses, commercial buildings, church, manse, church hall, blacksmith shop, and post office. Not much remains today except the grand ruins of Cooey Costello's unexpectedly sophisticated hotel, with its lacy verandas and main door with transom and sidelights, which is now being restored.

The Reddens, the Sneddens, the Raycrofts, and the Monroes opened their "foine" stopping-places along the Line, as did the Foys at Foymount, the Kirwans and the Dealys at Hopefield, the Jeffries at Harriet's Corners, the Plaunts at Plaunt's Mountain, the Payettes and the Costellos at Brudenell. But the Costellos went "real fancy"; they built in frame, put stained-glass sidelights and fantail on their front door, and Victorian lace on their huge verandas. One day, it is said, a team of oxen came down the Opeongo with a cargo that brought everybody out of their houses for a "look-see." Costello's grand piano had finally arrived from Ottawa. And it is said to be sitting there in the parlour yet, a grand and ancient ruin within a grand and ancient ruin.

Reputedly sons of Irish chieftains with a love of horses in their blood, it was logical that the Costellos would build a race track near their famous stopping-place. And, just up the road a little way from the Costellos, the Haggerty Boys, "the best fiddlers the Valley has ever known," decided to put their barns to better use than as horse stalls and hay storage. According to Valley legend (today completely denied by Haggertys), one barn became a famous dance hall and the other a gambling casino. Brudenell, legend would have it, became the early "sin bin" of the Opeongo, and from all over the Valley, from Fort Coulonge and Pembroke, from Shawville and Quyon, from Perth and Pakenham, from Carleton Place and Carp, the young bucks with their "fast hot" horses and their lily-white girls came to place their bets and "swing their partners."

St. Mary's Roman Catholic Church was built by the settlers in the 1870s. The "new" cemetery is to the west of the church on the same side of the road; the "old" cemetery is directly across the road to the west side of the "new" manse and, behind that, the "old" manse, now the church hall and probably the oldest building on the site. The old cemetery has stones dating back to 1815 and, except for one Payette memorial and another one in memory of the son of an Algonquin chief whose death occurred by drowning (probably on a river drive), the cemetery is a 100-percent chronicle of the lives of the Irish pioneers.

This is the country of the renowned storyteller Taddy Haggerty, the champion wit of the Opeongo Line. On the steps of St. Mary's Church one day a hundred years ago, Father Harrington, or Father Cormac, or Father Dowdall soundly scolded Taddy Haggerty for keeping the parishioners of Brudenell away from holy things and standing outside on the church steps listening to Taddy tell stories and making them laugh.

Taddy Haggerty was born on the old Haggerty Farm on the Opeongo Line in 1864 and died there in 1969, aged 95. Twenty years later I was able to collect Taddy Haggerty stories from succeeding generations all along the Line — the Sheridans, the Jessops, the Walthers, Father John Haas, Mrs. June Winiarski, Father John May of Vinton. Indeed, Bill Kehoe of CBC Radio in Ottawa gave me the name of a man in Sudbury who could tell me more Taddy Haggerty stories.

❡ STORY

Mrs. Jane Winiarski of Quadville told me this story:

Up in Brudenell old Mr. Wingle got married for the second time. He got hold of another old lady, and married her, and he was really blowing about the second woman he'd got. Oh, she was a good worker! And she could keep a fire on. And work in the barn. And milk the cows. And mostly he was telling everybody what a good cook she was. Oh, she was a good cook! And one time old Mr. Wingle was talking to Taddy Haggerty on the steps of the church at Brudenell and he said, 'I tell you, Taddy, I got a fine woman this time. She's a great cook. I tell you she can make a meal out of nothing.'

"And Taddy says to Wingle, 'And by God, she'd often have to do that!' "

✽

The Opeongo Line proceeds into the Opeongo Mountains, offering the explorer scenic panoramas of Opeongo country that become increasingly beautiful as the road progresses from Davidson's Corners and the Lake Clear country to the hilly, wooded high country of Wilno and Barry's Bay. Indeed, in the stretch from Brudenell to Barry's Bay, the scenery is likely to provide strong competition for the log building complexes along the road.

Hopefield

The irony of this name is manifest in the landscape. Hopefield obviously was a sawmill centre, and even today a small sawmill, lumber sheds, and piles of lumber remain. The old Hopefield farmstead, located at mile 57 of the Opeongo Line, is reported by local historians to have been a stopping-place. And this is quite likely since its proportions, 35 by 26 feet, is larger than the usual 20 by 18 of a typical log farmhouse. Gingerbread detailing on the veranda and a centre door with side and transom lights further indicates a commercial use.

DIRECTIONS

Continue on along the Opeongo until you come to a T marked "Daly Road, Opeongo Line and Wilno." At this point the Opeongo Line follows the signs to Wilno. Along this stretch are two outstanding deserted log building complexes with some of the very highest of the Opeongo Hills as background. At Wilno, an early Polish settlement, you come to major Highway No. 60. Follow this road into Barry's Bay. Along the way, do not miss making this roadside stop on *Shrine Hill* near the Roman Catholic church to savour one of the great views of the Ottawa Valley. The side roads, hillsides, and even hilltops are dotted with log farmsteads built by the Poles — and sometimes the Germans — but they are of a later date than those along the first section of the Opeongo.

This is another story from the late Tom Murray:

One of the greatest men this country ever produced was John Wesley Dafoe of Combermere. I can tell you a story about that. There was a schoolteacher named Gibson teaching in Madawaska. He was educated and had a good library of books. He went to Barry's Bay in the winter of 1880, drank some bad liquor there, and died. The trustees were desperate for another teacher and after a time they found a replacement in young John Wesley Dafoe. He arrived by birchbark canoe at McLachlin's Depot in Barry's Bay and joined some shantymen who were walking in to Madawaska. One of these uneducated shantymen was John Hunt, the blacksmith from Mount St. Patrick. John was a great blacksmith but he hadn't had much schooling and it was always said in this country that the only formal education of any kind that John Hunt ever had was that walk to Madawaska with John Wesley Dafoe!''

✳

Barry's Bay

Most heritage buildings in this town, such as Murray's Hudson's Bay Trading Post, are wiped from the townscape now. But the entrance to Barry's Bay is distinguished by the Railway Station, the water tower, and the Balmoral Hotel, all vintage.

Dating from about 1900, the *Railway Station* reflects the development of Barry's Bay from a hamlet on "the Blueberry Plains" into a town prospering from its position on the Ottawa, Arnprior, and Parry Sound Railway. The station is not a frontier-type square-timber building but a well-detailed version of a southern Ontario standard railway station. It is being put to good alternative use now as a social centre for senior citizens.

The wooden water tower near the station is one of the very few left in the country and is distinguished by a wooden support system and a round wooden tank.

One of the few ancient wooden watering holes left in the Valley — they burn down at the rate of about one a year — the old *Balmoral Hotel* across from the station throngs with the ghosts of

BARRY'S BAY RAILWAY STATION

*Once a key station on the Ottawa–Arnprior–Parry Sound railway
line, this station now serves as a senior citizen's meeting place.*

the great characters of the Barry's Bay area — lumbermen Murray and O'Manick (particularly the legendary Tom Murray), J.R. Booth on his way up to the Madawaska limits, John Egan on his way to the Egan Estates; strongmen Bunker Joe Helferty, Big Bob Foy, Joe Corrigan Prince (he was called Corrigan because he was as big as the Corrigans), Mike O'Leary, Hiram Holmes of Kemptville, the Maloneys, and the Culhanes of Mount St. Patrick.

¶ S T O R Y

Jack Jewel of Fort Coulonge gave me this story:

One time this old lad from Brudenell was travelling around with his brother-in-law, a visiting priest from Ottawa. The old lad from Brudenell was showing the holy father some of the major sights on the Opeongo Line. When they passed the Balmoral Hotel in Barry's Bay, the old man said to the priest, 'See that building over there?'

" 'Yes, I do,' said the priest, 'and it looks mighty like a hotel to me.'

" 'Not at all,' said the old lad from Brudenell. 'It is a holy shrine.'

" 'Now, how can that be?' asked the priest.

" 'Well,' said the old lad from Brudenell, 'it's this way. If you sit out here across from the hotel about two o'clock in the afternoon, you'll see all sorts of dishabilitated people in great pain going in on crutches and canes. And if you're here about five o'clock, you'll see them all coming out jolly as can be, joking and laughing and singing, with their canes tucked under their arms and their crutches over their shoulders.' "

*

Bark Lake Post Office

Located at mile 69 of the Opeongo Line, the Bark Lake Post Office is situated on a little loop of Highway No. 60, north of Bark Lake. This site is a unique heritage resource on the Opeongo, for the log buildings on the site remain intact and include the only log post office on the Line. Now used as a summer home, it has never been renovated, only well maintained. North of the post office are two well-maintained square-timber buildings.

DIRECTIONS

You can return home the way you came along the Opeongo Line, catching the hills in the sunset, or you can take the quick way east from Barry's Bay down Highway No. 60 to No. 17 straight into Ottawa and the Queensway. Or you can take No. 60 into Eganville, have something to eat at the Granary there, and head on down No. 60 through Douglas to Renfrew and No. 17. Or from Eganville, No. 41 takes you to Dacre (it's a beautiful road), thence into Renfrew, and back to Ottawa. Another option, if you have the time, is to stay overnight in Renfrew and from there launch your tour of Pembroke and the white-water country, described in the next chapter, by heading to Cobden on Highway No. 17.

Chapter 8

PEMBROKE
and the
WHITE-WATER COUNTRY

Preamble

The towns of Cobden, Beachburg, Westmeath, La Passe, Foresters Falls, Pembroke, Petawawa, Chalk River, and Deep River are all situated in Renfrew County, but the "White-Water Country" around Pembroke is so endowed with beauty, so rich in things to see and do, so permeated with the spirit of history, that I feel it deserves a tour of its own. As a matter of fact, it is easily more than a one-day tour, so you might like to consider places to camp on the water, or find a bed and breakfast in the area, or choose a hotel-motel accommodation. You might also consider selecting only parts of the tour you can accomplish in one-day explorations. The fastest way to start out is on Highway No. 17, toward Arnprior.

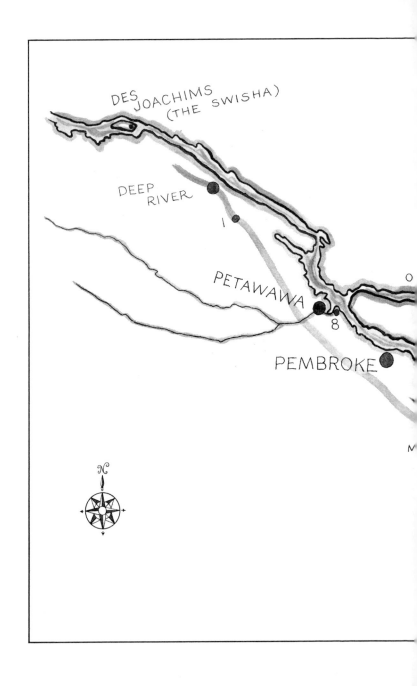

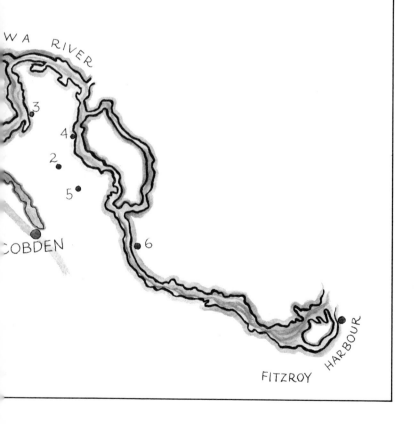

1 CHALK RIVER
2 BEACHBURG
3 WESTMEATH
4 LA PASSE
5 FORESTERS FALLS
6 PORTAGE DU FORT
7 ALLUMETTE LAKE
8 PETAWAWA POINT

W A RIVER

3

4

2

5

COBDEN

6

FITZROY HARBOUR

Cobden

A charming little service-centre town on Muskrat Lake and Highway No. 17, Cobden now might be called "the gateway to White-Water Country" — and to the Owl, the Whitewater, and the Ottawa Wilderness Tours rafting companies on the Ottawa River. All roads east from Cobden and No. 17 lead toward this rafting paradise. Right on the highway in the centre of Cobden sits one of the loveliest stopovers in the Upper Valley: Cobden Park, distinguished by virgin white pines towering over the town and by Muskrat Lake, providing picnic, swimming, toilet, and camping facilities. If you haven't packed a picnic, you can wine and dine directly across from the riverside park at the Village Pantry Roadhouse Restaurant on Dorothy Turner's "handcrafted" meals, either in her downstairs flower-filled dining room or upstairs in her "local pub," where, if you are lucky, you might catch some of the town characters "in their cups" and telling stories.

¶ STORY

One of the most famous sons of the Pembroke area was M.J. Heney, who became known in the Yukon and the North as "The Irish Prince" and "The Prince of the North." His parents on their pioneer farm north of Pembroke being unable to finance him to university, Heney, as a boy of fifteen, hitched his star to the CPR, then stretching its steel across Canada. He studied trigonometry by correspondence course in the railroad construction camps and became a great surveyor. He made his millions as one of Canada's greatest railway builders, and was responsible for the construction of the White Pass and the Yukon Railway. He was the hero of Rex Beach's book *The Iron Trail*. He died alone at 45 in his own private solarium overlooking San Francisco Bay.

HISTORY

Champlain found Indians on the present-day site of Cobden. His brief 1613 description of that stopover gives us the first glimpse of agriculture in the Upper Ottawa country: "Near this lake there is a settlement of Indians who till the ground and reap corn. The chief is named Nibachis, who came with his band to see us, marvelling that we had been able to pass the rapids and bad trails to reach them — they showed me their gardens and fields, where they have corn." On Highway No. 17 at Cobden a Historic Sites Plaque marks the discovery of Champlain's astrolabe — or what is thought to have been Champlain's astrolabe. If Canadians want to see this astrolabe, they can go to the Museum of the New York Historical Society, 170 Central Park West, New York City.

❡ STORY

In 1967 George Edward Lee was helping to clear land for Captain Overman of the Union Forwarding and Railway Company. As Lee was moving logs with a team of oxen named Buck and Brin, a log rolled over, disturbing a thick bed of moss, which rolled back like a blanket. There on the ground Lee saw a "round yellow thing, nine or ten inches across, with figures on it and an arm across it, pointed at one end and blunt at the other."

According to Lee's story, he "gave the compass to Pa and he put it on a stump. Just then Captain Overman came along to see how the work was going and old Captain Cowley was with him, Pa showed them the compass and they took it away and Pa said they promised to give me $10 for it, but I never got a farthing nor saw hide nor hair of the compass since."

✳

White Water Artisan Tours

Cobden promotes the White Water Artisan Tours during the second weekend in May, when the land is a-greening, and during the first weekend in October, when the autumn leaves are at their best in the Valley. If you would like to do the tour by bus, call Gilchrist Bus lines or Cobden Bus lines. If you prefer a self-guided tour using your own transportation, you can begin and end the tour wherever you choose. Here are some of the places you will visit on the White Water Artisan Tour:

At *Spokeshave Crafts* ash splint baskets, snowshoes, canoe paddles, and chairs are all handmade in traditional ways from the finest forest materials. Follow Main Street in Cobden to the United Church, turn left to 14 Gould Street.

At *Wood 'N Things*, R.R. #1, Cobden, Kent Graham does fine furniture and cabinet work, custom-crafted from local and imported hardwoods, while Lynn Graham makes wheel-thrown stoneware.

At *4 Kids*, R.R. #3, Cobden, Beth Beaupré custom-designs and makes children's clothing, and will do the same for adults if they wish. She does everything from bunting bags to smocked christening gowns, from crib quilts to dresses for girls and play clothes for boys. Watch for signs off Highway No. 17, just before the Flea Market.

At *Stonefurrow Art Glass* down the same road, Clayton Rollins works in stained glass, making original or custom-designed windows, panels, lamps, family crests, etc.

This artisan tour also takes you into the heart of the white-water country, to La Passe, Foresters Falls, Beachburg, and Westmeath. At Foresters Falls in an old restored Victorian mansion, *Joanne Pratt* in her studio creates dolls, soft sculpture, jewelry, and hats, all from her own unique and original designs.

The Beachburg Inn Antiques, at 161 Main Street, Beachburg, is run by Ken Fink, a retired Ottawa businessman. His fine antique shop features silver, china, stained glass, and furniture. Up the street from the antique shop, at 182 Main Street, you'll find *T'N'T Trivia*, owned by fabric artists Cathie Timm and Judy Tomlinson, who create a wide variety of items for every occasion. They also sell gifts and handcrafts, both local and from across Canada.

On the Ottawa River at La Passe, *Helen's Studio Gallery* features original watercolours of rural scenery and buildings by Helen Schruder.

Big Bend Pottery, at Westmeath, has a splendid view over the Ottawa River. Artisan Ben Zettler works there in his studio, crafting custom-made coffee mugs, candle holders, pitchers, sugar bowls, vases, flower pots, etc.

White-Water Rafting

In its course from northern Quebec at Lake Capimichigama down to the St. Lawrence River at Montreal, the Ottawa River performs many tumultuous feats over precipices and heights of land, creating rapids and sets of rapids that have captured and held man's fancy for decades. An Ottawa Valley poet, Fred Coyne, put all the romantic names of these rapids into verse in his "The Riverman's Fancy":

The seven chutes of Calumet
Are flooded deep from view,
And muffled is the rapid's roar,
Along the Rocher Fendu.
Since hydro power dams have stemmed
The Ottawa, to change,
Portage du Fort's rock-riven shore
Is soundless now, and strange.

Old Devil's Elbow crooks unseen;
Grand Sable lifts no sound;
Gray Mountain Chute is deadly mute
Like D'Argis Rapids, drowned;
Wild cataracts from Lac Coulonge
Lie listless in a lake
Where once the lunging River's plunge
Made rocky ravines quake.

Des Chats, Chenaux, la Rocher Fendu,
Des Joachims and La Cave;
Those waters leapt the Laurentides,
Are docile now and suave;
But somehow from the whirling wheels
Of hydro plants we hear
The power song we know belonged
To Chutes of yesteryear.

Many of the great rapids and chutes on the Ottawa River have been depleted by the building of dams at Fitzroy Harbour, at Portage-du-Fort, and at Des Joachims (The Swisha). The Rocher Fendu rapids, as they sweep around the east shore of Calumet

Island, remained an untouched, unspoiled wilderness section until a few years ago when entrepreneurs realized the potential of this section for white-water rafting, already a popular adventure in the United States. Three rafting companies in Canada now offer tours down the Ottawa. Today, all along the river where once real explorers and real rivermen met the challenges, today pseudo-adventurers by the hundreds from all over the world come creaming down in rubber rafts wearing life preservers.

<h2 style="text-align:center">¶ STORY</h2>

Only one man alive today has ever shot the Rocher Fendu in a canoe — and that was by mistake. Bob Fenton of Sand Bay, Quebec, tells his story:

I started off at Moorhead's and stopped in at Davidson for supplies. One old lad there asked me where I was going and I told him I was canoeing down to Portage-du-Fort. He looked at me in surprise and drawled out, 'Well, I don't envy you that trip. Stay close to the Quebec side.' Looking back now, I remember that several people warned me: 'Stay close to the Quebec side.' But nobody told me what lay ahead of me. I thought my route would take me a week, but I shot down so fast it only took me a day!

"Along my way I came to an overflow dam with a 10- or 12-foot drop and I portaged around this one and got back into my canoe. Ahead of me I could hear a sound like a heavy breeze. The sound became a roar and then without any warning I was into the nine roosters' tails of the Rocher Fendu. I made it through one, portaged around another, got back into the water again, and tried to make my way down and through. My supplies and equipment were lost. The canoe was torn to shreds. The final rooster's tail dumped me, sucked me down into a whirlpool, and tore me across the rocks. Bleeding and dazed, I landed in at where Consolidated Bathurst is today. The last cottages had just been sold and the last cottagers were packing up. They gave me help but couldn't believe my story. Nobody had ever shot the Rocher Fendu before. Today it is the site of the Ottawa Whitewater Rafting business on the Ottawa, but now the 100,000 visitors a year come down in rubber rafts with life preservers on! My only real regret is that I had shot through the site of a million-dollar business and didn't recognize it!"

Wilderness Tours

The largest and most comprehensive of the triumvirate of rafting companies performing at the Rocher Fendu, Wilderness Tours offers one- and two-day trips on the Ottawa at their site on two different runs: the middle or Quebec channel, and its sister, Ontario's main channel. Extras at the site include sand beaches for swimming and sunning, wind surfing, kayaking, canoeing, and camping. Rafter's, a new restaurant complex near Foresters Falls, provides facilities for wining and dining, a gift shop, a conference centre, and, in the off season, scheduled weekend events from live-theatre-with-dinner to the wild and woolly Hunter's Ball in November.

Owl Rafting

Owl is Eastern Canada's oldest rafting company. Owl's equipment is the very latest and lightest available world wide. Your trip includes four to five hours of white-water rafting, breakfast and lunch, free camping, wind surfing, canoeing, and kayaking.

Ottawa Whitewater Rafting

More family-oriented than the others, Ottawa Whitewater Rafting offers all-inclusive vacation packages, cabin rentals, a children's day camp, and recreational activities for all.

Pembroke

Pembroke, as well as most of its umbrella towns, is blessed with not only "water, water, everywhere" but also with the presence of the Quebec-side mountains; indeed, just above Pembroke the mountains come so close to the Ottawa River that they "fall into the sea." Dozens of picturesque islands add to the beauty of the Ottawa River in this part of its 700-mile course to the St. Lawrence.

Below Pembroke, the Ottawa River performs one of its swiftest, most awe-inspiring plunges down to the flatlands around Ottawa, leaping over plateaus and precipices, swirling around Allumette and Calumet islands, transforming the whole area into white-water country. Boat launches, boat rentals, boat tours, and marinas dot the area, making it possible for the traveller with even a limited income to explore the mighty Ottawa.

From Pembroke to The Swisha (Des Joachims) lies one of the most beautiful stretches of the river, arrayed with virgin forests running down the mountains into the sea, untouched beaches, unexplored bays — particularly on the Quebec side of the river. Owl Rafting, Wilderness Tours, and Ottawa Whitewater Rafting might be said to be the Ottawa Valley's first international tourist attractions. Every year thousands of people from all over the world now come to the white-water country to shoot the rapids on the Ottawa.

Drawing on thousands of potential buyers from both sides of the river — it is said to service over 60,000 people — Pembroke itself is a shopping mecca fulfilling every conceivable need from *haute couturière* clothes to a wide range of imported cheeses, from rare books to vintage wines. A pretty little city on the water, Pembroke has many of the amenities of a big city: an array of clubs and organizations, recreational facilities, an arts council, live theatre, movie houses, and places to wine and dine — a few of them, like Treadles, making their way into *Where to Eat in Canada*. All of these "big-city" aspects *with* the added bonus of the leisurely pace and country friendliness of the village scene and *without* the hectic pace and high living of the metropolis are features combining to make Pembroke, like Perth and Kingston, a "somewhat retirement town."

HISTORY

The first tree felled upon the present-day site of Pembroke was cut down by Peter White on May 24, 1828. Before his arrival, White had already decided he would become a lumberman; his action that May day set the tone for Pembroke as a major lumbering town in the Valley.

Born in Scotland on Hogmanay (New Year's Eve day) in 1794, White joined the Mercantile Marine during the War of 1812, and in 1813 came with Commodore Sir James Yeo and 500 officers and

BOOTH MANSION, PEMBROKE

This mansion on Main Street represents the grand buildings constructed with "Old Pembroke Money." The town is rich with such baronial structures.

men to man the British fleet on Lake Ontario. At the end of the war White retired from naval service and came to the Ottawa Valley to engage in lumbering.

Prior to the momentous tree felling on the site of Pembroke, White had already been lumbering in the Lower Valley. His partner there disappeared with the proceeds of the sale of their year's timber, leaving White to pay the firm's debts. This he did, but was left penniless. Undeterred, White left his wife and two children in Aylmer and started up the Ottawa Valley in 1827 to prospect further for timber stands. In the winter of 1827–28, he walked from Aylmer to Pembroke and back again, from Aylmer to Maitland on the St. Lawrence to do some business, and then again from Aylmer to Pembroke — a total of 500–600 miles. Finally in the spring of 1828 White packed his belongings, his pregnant wife, their children, and their supplies into a canoe and began the journey up the Ottawa from Aylmer to Pembroke, loading and unloading for the portages around the rapids, spending the nights in the bush in black-fly and mosquito season.

It is significant that White had no intention of settling as a farmer. He immediately began lumbering and was joined by James Carney and then by two brothers, Michael and Donald McNeil. White began to gather about him the workmen necessary for survival in his lumbering business, and he also recruited a blacksmith, a sleigh maker, a harness maker, and a shoemaker. As well, White opened a small store and established the first schoolhouse.

Following White into the lumbering business were the Dunlops, John Arunah, and Hugh John Supple, who moved in from Allumette Island to become a wealthy lumberman. Fortunes were to be made by Christopher O'Kelly, Richard White, M. O'Meara, the Moffats, the Bells, the MacKays, the Heenans, the Frasers, the Pinks, the Edwardses, the Murrays, the Mackies, and many others.

By the time of his death in 1858 at the age of 84, Peter White, Sr., had lived to see Pembroke incorporated as a village with a population of 80. The town was decreed the county seat of Renfrew County in 1866.

This intrepid lumbering pioneer set the tone and the lifestyle for the future of Pembroke. From the beginning it was a society deeply overlaid with layers of lumbering money and later, when the timber barons themselves had died off, with "Old Pembroke

Money" passed on to and being lived on by descendants of the timber barons. All along MacKay and Pembroke streets and in the quadrangle made by those two streets the lumbering people of Pembroke built their baronial mansions, entertained officers from Petawawa, and held galas in their splendid ballrooms.

❦ S T O R Y

This story came from the late Mrs. S.M. Robertson of Ottawa and Pembroke:

Pembroke was always gay. There was all that money and then there was the military. It was endless parties and military euchres and balls and picnics and cruises down the Ottawa.

"I can tell you about another one of my most vivid memories of growing up in Pembroke. Now, Frances Murray was a very pretty girl. They were Roman Catholics. Her father was Joe Murray, later MP. Her brother Joe married Estelle O'Brien from Renfrew; she was the daughter of M.J. O'Brien, the famous lumber and mining magnate. Anyhow, I was just coming 'on the scene' in Pembroke and I remember seeing Frances Murray's younger half-sister at a Christmas house party at the Bedores'. Dr. Bedore was French from France. He never practiced; he lived on his wife's money. She was an O'Meara from Portage-du-Fort.

"The Bedores had this lovely, lovely house with a long drawing room — the whole end wall one huge full-length mirror in which you could watch yourself dancing. Mrs. Bedore's beautiful white and gold harp always stood in front of that mirror. They had this lovely Christmas party and they always entertained beautifully — their daughters were all my friends — and really, I never sat at a table where — the girls always served, you know, at a supper party — where you always felt that it was a real act of hospitality and that everything had been especially arranged *just for you.*"

✳

Underneath this layer of 12 bridesmaids to a wedding and living rooms lined with mirrors from France, Pembroke was a shanty town with sometimes hundreds of teams moving along its streets to the lumber camps in the wildernesses around and about it.

From its five shantymen's hotels moved in and out a constant stream of often larger-than-life men, taking supplies to the camps, going up to work, stopping over on "the Drive," arranging to spend their winter's pay, aching to settle a score.

❡ S T O R Y

The late Alec McDermid of Burnstown gave me this story:

Oh yes, the MacNabs were big fellows! But there was another one I remember up on Calumet Island, there near Fort William, name of Mike Jennings. That was Jennings country. There was Mike and Ray and Cyril. But Mike was the strong one. Mike Jennings could hold two horseshoes in one hand and four of us in the lumber camp couldn't pull them apart. He didn't carry an ounce of fat and weighed 250 pounds.

"I can tell you a story about Mike Jennings. One time they were loading horses at Pembroke. It was half-past ten at night and I guess it was Saturday night, shopping night, drinking night, because there were people on the streets and people in the hotels. Well, anyhow, this Mike Meighen from Pembroke was loading horses loaded — not drunk but very happy. He had a team of horses that weighed about 3800 pounds and he decided to play tricks with them; started chasing one of them down the street ahead of him and then over onto the sidewalk. People started screaming and running. There was a woman with a baby carriage in the way. Mike Jennings ran up and grabbed those horses and he didn't lead them off the sidewalk or pull them off the sidewalk — he just *took* them off the sidewalk, *lifted* them off the sidewalk!"

✳

Festival of Swallows

Each summer the city of Pembroke welcomes home Canada's largest concentration of martins and swallows. From mid-July to late August, at sunrise and sunset, over 100,000 swallows perform spectacular aerobatic displays as they leave and then return to their roosts along the historic Ottawa River.

While Pembroke's swallow roost is often compared to that of San Juan, Capistrano, the swallows of each location have definite characteristics of their own. The flock of San Juan returns faithfully each year on March 19 to herald the arrival of spring in California. In contrast, small groups of Pembroke's huge flock begin to roost in early June. By mid-July a small stand of willows near the city's marina has become home to an impressive flock, which reaches its peak size during the first two weeks of August.

All six Eastern Canadian swallow species are represented within the flock, the Tree Swallow being most predominant. The Barn and Bank swallows and the Purple Martin are also well represented, while the Cliff and Rough-winged swallows are fewer in number.

Just as these birds welcome the arrival of the summer season, so their departure signals the end to long sunny days. With the passage of each cold front the number of swallows gradually declines until the roost is finally abandoned by early September.

The swallows leave the roost daily at about 30 minutes before sunrise, returning each evening at about 30 minutes before sunset. Not many visitors are up early enough to view the flock's spectacular departure, but each evening large crowds gather along the breakwater of the Pembroke Marina, which offers an excellent view of the aerial performance of the returning swallows.

A highlight for both new and seasoned birdwatchers is to spot the elusive merlin, a small falcon that regularly preys on swallows and is one of the few birds capable of doing so in mid-air.

According to the Canadian Wildlife Service, the size and the diversity of this flock make it unique among recorded swallow roosts. It provides one of the major spectacles of swallow migration in Canada and captivates the attention of tourists, conservation groups, and the national media. Members of the Pembroke bird club are often at the marina breakwater in the evening to answer questions and distribute guides.

Annual Old-Time Fiddling
and Step Dancing Competition

Since its successful introduction in 1975, the annual Labour Day Weekend Pembroke and Area Old-Time Fiddling and Step Dancing Competition has become one of the most renowned in North America, drawing fans and contestants back year after year from

213

all over Canada and the United States. The two-day event includes competitions of traditional old-fashioned fiddling and step dancing with trophies and cash prizes amounting to close to $5,000.

While the Pembroke Memorial Centre is the official site of all organized competitions and events, musically minded campers and their families can get even greater entertainment value by booking into beautiful Riverside Park, where spontaneous displays of old-time music and step dancing are enjoyed and applauded throughout the entire weekend. Situated on the shores of the Ottawa River, this municipally owned campsite is located within city limits, providing campers with electrical hookups, comfort stations, firewood, ice, and laundry facilities. There is also an abundance of comfortable accommodation and highly recommended restaurants for visitors to enjoy.

Artists' studios, wood carvers' outlets, craft shops, and antiquaries that surround Pembroke lure browsers and buyers into and out of town during the Competition.

Other Pleasures Around Pembroke

The old Galligan house, a landmark on Pembroke's main street for over 150 years, now houses *Heritage House*. Here you will find hand-crafted quilts, stained glass, pottery, weaving, and smocking from the finest of the Ottawa Valley craftsmen and artisans.

Four miles east of Pembroke in an old farmhouse on Mud Lake Road, you can visit *The Calico Cat*, which offers Valley crafts of all kinds, Canadiana, and collectibles. Follow the signs from Old Highway No. 17 or exit County Road No. 24, the White Water Road, from the Pembroke bypass.

At *Pine Ridge Park and Resort*, a well-established campground site, the *Bell Loft Crafts Shop* features the work of local artisans and gifts of all kinds. Four miles west of Pembroke turn off No. 17 at County Road No. 26. At Airport Road turn right and continue on this road to the Ottawa River.

A great family-oriented wayside stopover is *Gourmet Farms*, located at the corner of Black Bay Road and Highway No. 17, a few minutes west of Pembroke. Leading attractions here are an ice cream parlour and the fresh-picked local strawberries, raspberries, wild blueberries, and vegetables. Homemade from the kitchens comes fudge of all kinds, maple syrup and maple candy, local honey and comb honey, pies, jams, pickles. Gifts and novelties include unusual T-shirts and genuine Indian moccasins.

Boating on the Ottawa

For those who like wilderness, unspoiled beaches, clean water, and uncrowded anchorages, tours from the Pembroke Marina offer unlimited opportunities.

Pembroke is located on Allumette Lake, a 15-square-mile body of water excellent for day sailing. The cruising area is detailed on Chart No. 1553. Navigational aids such as buoys and lighthouses exist throughout the entire area. The marina offers mooring for over 100 boats. Pembroke Community Services Department manages the marina which, during the summer season, operates daily, has 24-hour surveillance, and is well lit. Facilities include toilets, pump-out gas, ice, fast foods, and bait. Downtown Pembroke is just two blocks away.

Although the marina does not have an on-site hoist, there are several cranes available from local industry. There is an excellent launching ramp at the marina, and electricity is available for repairs.

For racing enthusiasts, there are three major regattas, one of which is hosted by the Pembroke Sailing Association. Within the local cruising area are many points of interest, including the Canadian Forces Base Petawawa Yacht Club, just 15 miles west of Pembroke — a modern facility that welcomes visitors. It is licensed by the Liquor Licensing Board of Ontario and refreshments and meals are available.

Fort William, just beyond Petawawa, was the most southerly trading post of the Hudson's Bay Company. The trader's home is indeed still inhabited. An old hotel, located at the beach site, offers cold refreshments and meals, and a number of islands and beaches in the area provide scenic anchorages. (See also Chapter 5 for more information on Fort William.)

Proceeding west, the next stop is Oiseau Rock. This popular beach/anchorage is accessible only by water and is one of the most important natural landmarks of the area. The reward for a 25-minute climb to the top is a 180-degree panoramic view of the Ottawa Valley and a cool dip in its 10-acre crystal-clear, spring-fed lake.

Deep River Yacht and Tennis Club offers visitors a variety of amenities, and at present a new marina is being planned. Shopping is within walking distance, while a number of anchorages lie across the river. Beach facilities are maintained by the River Recreation Improvement Association.

Big and Little Presqu'ile are beautiful sheltered bays that offer perhaps the most scenic anchorages located in this area. A few miles west of Deep River is Rapides des Joachims (The Swisha), where it is possible to tie up to the Federal Wharf overnight. Adjacent to the wharf are several hotels that operate regularly. Because of the power dam located at Des Joachims, it is impossible to proceed beyond this point.

Farther Up River

Petawawa

The next step up Highway No. 17 from Pembroke is Petawawa. Since 1905, when the Royal Canadian Horse and Garrison Artillery fired their 12-pounder guns over the Petawawa sand dunes under the direction of Camp Commander Lieutenant-Colonel G.H. Ogilvie, Petawawa soldiers have been part of the scene in the Upper Ottawa Valley on both sides of the river. In times of depression, these soldiers have given the area regular pay cheques, and at other times squired the girls to the dances and provided some of the great barroom fights of Valley history.

Barry's Bay and Kazubazua were first considered for a military base before an order-in-council in 1905 empowered the Minister of Militia and Defence to acquire at Petawawa the necessary land for artillery practice — the properties of 150 settlers, totalling 22,432 acres, along with 52,000 acres of Crown lands, making a total area of 116 square miles.

Petawawa Military Museum

If you are interested in obsolete military memorabilia, or your children would enjoy seeing historic aircraft and a wide variety of military equipment used by our armed forces since the beginning of the twentieth century, then visit the Canadian Airborne Forces Museum and CFB Petawawa Military Museum. There are both indoor and outdoor displays describing 40 years of Canadian Airborne Forces history and the 80-year history of Camp Petawawa itself. There are picnic facilities on the site.

Petawawa National Forestry Institute

As an antidote to the planning for destruction at the Petawawa Military Camp Base, close by you can visit a site dedicated to the ecological preservation of our natural world: the Petawawa National Forestry Institute.

You can spend a whole "greening-of-the-earth" day at the Forest Visitor Centre, experiencing the 100-kilometre trip through this national research forest, having an adventure into nature learning and history. World-renowned forestry research has been conducted here since 1918, and you can learn all about it either through walking tours or self-guided tours in your own car. There are outdoor exhibits and a marvellous two-storey tree house that every young child will want to take home. A picnic area, a sandy beach for swimming, and a public boat launch are available free of charge.

Also nearby, at Petawawa Point, is a magnificent Ottawa River beach. One of the earliest watering places for monied Pembroke, the beach has a number of very old heritage cottages.

Chalk River

Farther up Highway No. 17 you come to Chalk River. As most Canadians — and even some Americans — probably know, this is the site of the Atomic Energy of Canada plant.

When construction began on the shores of the Ottawa River in 1944, shrouded in secrecy as the project was, local residents speculated widely on the nature of the new industry; but, according to Canadian Press reports of the times, it was generally held that "the government was building a new synthetic rubber plant." On August 6, 1945, the Honorable C.D. Howe, then Minister of Munitions and Supply, hinted at disclosure of what the plant was really about by giving the press a statement: "Canadian scientists and Canadian institutions have played an intimate part and have been associated in an effective way with this great scientific development." He was referring, of course, to the first atomic bomb, which had just been dropped on Hiroshima, Japan.

Soon after Howe's oblique announcement, Dr. C.J. Mackenzie, then president of the National Research Council in Ottawa, was asked by reporters how he saw the new form of energy being used for peaceful purposes. His response was premonitory and echoes down the years with new meaning: "We are at the beginning of an epoch-making period. At the time of the discovery of electricity, would the scientists then have envisaged things like Shipshaw [a hydroelectric station in Quebec then considered the "last word" in development]? Here is energy in a basic form never known. Where it will go to is open to the imagination."

Tours of the Chalk River Nuclear Laboratories

"Dedicated to researching and developing the peaceful applications of atomic energy," the Chalk River Nuclear Laboratories are open to the public. Free films and distribution of publications on nuclear energy precede guided bus and walking tours that take visitors from the educational displays at the Public Information Centre to close-up views of Canada's first nuclear research facilities.

Deep River

Sometimes called "Instant City," Deep River (also on Highway No. 17) is certainly "the youngest town of the Upper Ottawa Valley," created as it was in 1970. The town consists largely of scientists and related professionals and is frequently cited as a place "with more PhDs per acre than anywhere else in Canada." Paradoxically, it is filled with legends.

Many old rivermen claimed that the river at this stretch was "bottomless." They used to play tricks on strangers in town and on tourists who came to fish and hunt: they'd drop a great length of rope over the side of a boat with nothing on the end of it. Unweighted, the rope would of course go out and out, coiling on the bottom of the river. But to the uninitiated, the rope *did* seem endless and they would often turn pale at the thought of being on the surface of a "bottomless river."

If Deep River is a relative newcomer to the Valley, its name goes back at least 300 years, when the Sulpician priest Brehan de Galinée marked Rivière Creuse on his 1670 map. Explorer Chevalier de Troyes mentions Rivière Creuse in his journal of 1686. Land agent and canal dreamer Alexander Sherriff was at the site of the Deep River Reach as early as 1831. Provincial surveyor William Hawkins during his trip along the Ottawa in 1837 observed that there were "some scattered settlements along the Ottawa as far north as the Deep River." And in 1851 that ubiquitous lumberman John Egan reported that works such as dams and booms had been built on Chalk River as early as 1838 and on the Schyan River in Pontiac County from 1845.

❡ STORY

This story was told to me by Clarence McCullough of North Bay:

Moses Lamuir, an Algonquin chief, was one of the greatest fiddlers this country ever saw. And God! They were good rivermen! So light on their feet. So agile. And they'd leave the camp every Saturday night and go home in this big pointer up the lake, and one would play the fiddle and the rest of them row. Say, you never heard music like it in your life! Coming off that lake. Not a sound. Except the music. And all the loons for miles around would be hollering. You'd hear loons where there had never been loons before. And they could *all* play the fiddle. And the mouth organ. And the Jew's harp. And it was good music. Where they learned it, I don't know. Nor how."

✳

Because of its homogeneous upper-middle-class composition, Deep River tends to have many sophisticated amenities not usually found in a town of its size: beaches, fitness trails, tennis and squash courts, golf courses, yacht club, theatre, bookstore, and special festivals, clubs, and organizations of all kinds. It is the site of the Ottawa Valley Summer Orchestra Camp for young people. There are classical music concerts in the park in summertime, as well as "Art in the Park" craft fairs. The town sponsors a Cross River Swim competition and a triathlon.

Ryan's Campsite and Gifts

Another campsite-gift shop combination, Ryan's sells Canadian gifts and souvenirs, Indian moccasins and crafts, pottery, bric-a-brac, and furs. They specialize in Hudson's Bay parkas and Inuit sculptures. There is an air service from Ryan's for sightseeing the Valley and a free wildlife museum. Watch for the Teepee signs along Highway No. 17.

Log House Antiques

A little way off the main highway in a century-old log house, Log House Antiques sells gifts and crafts displayed as though used in the house. They specialize in Canadiana furniture, primitive tools, cast-iron utensils, china, glass, collectibles, as well as a wide selection of handmade dolls. They buy and sell. Watch for signs on Highway No. 17 near Deep River.

Ferguson's Stopping-Place

Many people grind to a stop at Deep River when they come to this beautifully restored complex of log buildings right on Highway No. 17. This cluster of classic nineteenth-century settlers' buildings was owned and lived in from 1930 to 1968 by old riverman John King, "one of them Kings from Lake Doré." Now preserved by Atomic Energy of Canada Limited, Ferguson's stopping-place was originally built by King's maternal grandfather, John Ferguson, "a Scotch Presbyterian who wouldn't sell you an egg on Sunday." Ferguson began running his business here about 1876, but prior to that, John Dowler was living on part of this land as early as 1857, where he sold liquor out of his Temperance Hotel.

¶ STORY

A few years before his death in 1968 John King described for me life in the stopping-places going up to the camps:

If you started at Pembroke there was a stopping-place right there in Pembroke called the Timmins Place. In fact, they're the same Timmins that are implicated in the Timmins Mine. You'd knock at the door and they knew you were coming in. Well,

FERGUSON'S STOPPING-PLACE, DEEP RIVER

*Atomic Energy Canada restored this complex of log buildings.
The site offers a prime example of an Ottawa Valley
stopping place circa 1860.*

if you wanted a meal they'd get it ready for you, but these portagers generally carried their own food in a box, cooked and all. They'd put their horses in a stable and fix them up. They'd have their blanket with them, rolled up, and they'd get them under their arm and their lunchbox and carry it in. Of course, it would be frozen, but they'd take it into the stove. They all had a teabag and they'd hand over their teabag and the women cooks would put it in a great big vessel — 10 cents to make the tea, and 25 cents to keep the team overnight."

✳

DIRECTIONS

The route back to Ottawa is along Highway No. 17, but once you reach Pembroke again, you can swing off to some of the back-roads you've already explored in the Valley or sample some new ones. (See Chapters 6 and 7.) If you haven't tried the north side of the river yet, this would be a good place to cross at Calumet Island and return to Ottawa along No. 148. (See Chapters 4 and 5.) You could even do the Ferryboat Junkets, starting at either Mohr's Landing on the south side of the river, or at Quyon on the north side, if you've already crossed the river at Calumet. (See Chapter 1.)

The possibilities are numerous and the choice is up to you!

Tourist Information Centres

Both Eastern Ontario and Western Quebec (l'Outaouais) are favoured with excellent tourist information centres. Before heading out on a tour of the Ottawa Valley, consider writing or calling a provincial or regional centre for detailed maps and brochures. Most municipalities in the Valley operate seasonal (Victoria Day to Labour Day) travel information centres. Drop by when you are in town and pick up brochures on local attractions and events. You might overhear yet another tall tale of life in the Ottawa Valley.

Eastern Ontario Travel Centres

PROVINCIAL

Ontario Ministry of Tourism and Recreation
Queen's Park
Toronto, Ontario
M7A 2E5
1-800-268-3735 *(English)*
1-800-268-3736 *(French)*

REGIONAL

Eastern Ontario Travel Association
209 Ontario Street
Kingston, Ontario
K7l 2Z1
1-613-549-3682

Western Quebec Travel Centres

PROVINCIAL

Tourisme-Québec
Ministère du Tourisme
C.P. 20 000
Québec, P.Q.
G1K 7X2

Association touristique de l'Outaouais
C.P. 2000 Succ. B
Hull, P.Q.
J8X 3Z2
1-819-778-2222

Capital (Ottawa) Travel Centres

Visitors and Convention Bureau
65 Elgin Street
Ottawa, Ontario
1-613-237-5158

National Capital Commission
14 Metcalfe Street
Ottawa, Ontario
1-613-239-5000

INDEX *of* PLACE NAMES

Aylmer 11, 77–106, 107, 110, 112–13
Angers 17, 20
Alfred 19
Alexandria 39, 58–59
Avonmore 41
Arnprior 7, 126, 139, 142, 143–48, 149, 175, 178, 199
Almonte 68, 88
Allumette Island 133, 137

Bonnechere Caves 166–167
Burnstown 152–54
Bark Lake 142, 169, 173, 196
Bryson 127–29
Bells Corners 17
Buckingham 18, 20, 21–23
Balaclava 7, 183
Balderson 61–62
Bristol 11, 121
Breckenridge 114
Barry's Bay 142, 169, 172, 185, 193, 194–96, 197, 216
Braeside 148, 176
Brudenell 169, 191–93, 196
Burritt's Rapids 173
Beachburg 199

Cobden 142, 197, 199, 202–05
Chapeau 133, 137
Calumet Island 125, 127–29, 205, 222
Calabogie 120, 142, 154–57, 183
Carp 17, 175, 191
Cumberland 11, 17, 19, 23–25
Como 19
Carlsbad Springs 25
Caledon Springs 25
Carillon 11, 36, 37
Cornwall 41, 42, 44, 55–58
Clayton 66
Crow Lake 76
Chats Falls 83, 111
Chelsea 101
Campbell's Bay 130
Castleford 148, 158, 175, 176–79, 181
Clontarf 169, 173, 187–88

Carleton Place 178, 191
Chalk River 199, 217–18, 219
Deux Rivières 11
Dunvegan 41, 42–44
Dalhousie Lake 70
Deschenes 83, 86, 87
Des Joachims (The Swisha) 107, 205, 208, 216
Deep River 142, 183, 216, 218–22
Douglas 142, 163–66, 167, 197
Dacre 163, 169, 172, 183–84, 185, 197

Eganville 92, 142, 167–68, 172, 183, 184, 197
Esmonde 169, 173, 185–86

Farrell's Landing 142, 169, 176–79
Fitzroy Harbour 83, 104, 11, 205
Finch 41
Fussifern 44
Franktown 69
Fort Coulonge 110, 131–32, 191, 196
Fort William 134, 215
Ferguslea 172, 180–81
Foresters Falls 199

Glengarry County 10, 37, 39–60, 142
Galetta 17, 175
Gatineau Point 17, 18
Glen Robertson 41
Glen Sandfield 41, 44
"Ghost Hill" 114–17
Griffith 142
Golden Lake 173

Hawkesbury 11, 19
Hudson 19
Herron's Mills 7, 63
Hopetown 64
Hull 80, 113
Hopefield 193

Johnstown (see Cornwall)

Kinburn 17

Kenyon 44
Killaloe 120, 142, 172
Kazabazua 130, 216

Lachine 19
Lochiel 44
Lancaster 59–60, 88
Lanark County 61–76
Lanark 63, 88
Luskville 111, 116, 117–18
Ladysmith 124
La Passe 199

Mohr's Landing 11, 12–17, 118, 222
Masson 11, 17, 20
McGregor Lake 19
Mayo 23–24
Montebello 27, 28–36
Maxville 39, 41, 43
Middleville 63
Mill of Kintail 66–67
Merrickville 69, 74–75
Mattawa 93
Mount St. Patrick 181, 183
McDougall 182
Magnetic Hill 184

Navan 25
Namur 27
Norway Bay 111, 121

Ottawa (Bytown) 10, 14, 19, 60, 104, 105–06, 137, 167, 168, 178, 197, 211–222
Opeongo Line 11, 142, 158, 168, 169–97
Oak Point 19
Otter Lake 124–25

Plaisance 17, 26–27
Papineauville 17, 26, 27
Pembroke 7, 22, 43, 88, 137, 139, 142, 191, 197, 199, 207–16, 220, 222
Pointe Fortune 11, 36–37
Perth 69–73, 88, 191
Prospect 69
Pontiac County 107–37
Portage–du–Fort 125–27, 205

Palmer's Rapids 142, 154
Pakenham 178, 191
Petawawa 199, 215, 216–17

Quyon 11, 12–17, 92, 110, 118–21, 191, 22
Quadville 192

Rockland 11, 26
Renfrew 7, 43, 142, 148, 149, 158–63, 167, 169, 172, 175, 179–80, 197
Richmond 69
Renfrew County 139–68, 151, 199

Shamrock 182
South March 17, 175
Sulphur Springs 25–26
Sarsfield 25
Ste–Andre–Avellin 36
Summerstown 41, 88
St. Elmo 43
Sharbot Lake 76
Shawville 111, 115–16, 121–24, 125, 191
Sheenboro 120, 136
Schwartz 124
Sand Point 148, 176
Storyland 163
Sand Bay 206

Thurso 11, 17, 26
Thorne Centre 124

Val des Monts 19
Vinoy 27
Val–Quesnel 36
Vankleek Hill 45
Vanbrugh 169, 190–91

Woodlawn 17
Williamstown 41, 45–55
Waba 149–52, 180
White Lake 149–52, 180
Wilno 169, 193
Westmeath 199, 204